Mrs. Major Vander Vliet

The Last Days Of PLANET EARTH

JERRY JOHNSTON

HARVEST HOUSE PUBLISHERS
Eugene, Oregon 97402

THE LAST DAYS OF PLANET EARTH

Copyright © 1991 by Harvest House Publishers
Eugene, Oregon 97402

Library of Congress Cataloging-in-Publication Data

Johnston, Jerry, 1959-
     The last days of planet earth / Jerry Johnston.
     ISBN 0-89081-901-7
     1. Bible—Prophecies.   I. Title.
BC347.2.J65   1991   91-14203
236′.9—dc20   CIP

Contents

◆ ━━━━━━ ◆

BOOKS BY JERRY JOHNSTON

It's Killing Our Kids: Teenage Alcohol Abuse and Addiction (Word)
The Edge of Evil: The Rise of Satanism in North America (Word)
Going All the Way: The Real World of Teens and Sex (Word)
Why Suicide? (Thomas Nelson Publishers)
The Last Days of Planet Earth (Harvest House)

VIDEOS BY JERRY JOHNSTON

It's Killing Our Kids (Word Video)
The Edge of Evil (Word Video)
Why Suicide? (Word Video)
Life Expose (Jerry Johnston Ministries)
The Cutting Edge (Word Video; a compilation of all four titles)

AUDIO MESSAGES BY JERRY JOHNSTON

Facts About Heaven: The Celestial City
The Coming Antichrist: Master Deceiver
A Trip to Hell
Interview with Teenage Satanic killer, Sean Sellers
Five Fatal Factors of Youth
What Is Repentance?
The Carnal Christian
Six Reasons Why Parents Lose Their Teens
The Holy Spirit
The Enemy Within
The Cross
Capture America/The Holiness of God
The Judgment Seat of Christ
Marks of a Christian
The Rapture
Satanism
What Happens at Death
My Conversion Story/Jerry's Life Story
Life Expose/High School Assembly Lecture
CNN Crossfire Debate with Satanist Paul Valentine
Thoughts on Soulwinning

New Age Movement: Spiritualism, Peace, or What?
It's Killing Our Kids: Youth Alcohol Abuse
Joyce Johnston Story: Deliverance from Alcoholism
Zaccheus—God's Thoughts About You

Foreword

I first met Jerry Johnston at our Billy Graham Conference of Itinerant Evangelists held in Amsterdam, July, 1986. Of the ten thousand assembled, he was, in my estimation, the most gifted and dedicated of the young evangelists present. He is an exemplary torchbearer for the upcoming generation. I was so impressed, that I asked him to take half of my teaching session during the conference. Filled with the zeal of the Holy Spirit and with a near-unique capacity to communicate the Gospel to high schoolers and collegians, he made a deep impression on those gathered.

Since then, everywhere I've gone people have talked of how Jerry Johnston has blessed people at high school assemblies and mega-church campaigns. His crusade in Toronto, Canada's largest evangelical congregation, People's Church (of which I am an Elder), was the most fruitful in decisions for Christ of any crusade in this quarter of the century. I went out to hear him address a thousand high schoolers in Scarborough, an industrial part of Toronto heavily populated with immigrants. You could have heard a pin drop, and that was only one of four assemblies he was addressing that day. He is indisputably a young man of God whose devotion to Christ has the healthiest possible balance of intelligence, integrity, and intensity.

I was so moved in reading Jerry's manuscript that I'm ordering copies by the thousands to give away to Canadians on my weekly TV telecast. *The Last Days of Planet Earth* is simply a must-read for anyone who is concerned about the downgrade conditions in our world. These conditions are leading to two impending events of unprecedented historic and eternal significance: the return of Jesus Christ and

Armageddon. Our society is very secular and even cynical, and demands hard facts about current events in the world today. The only valid road map for the convulsive times ahead is the changeless, accurate, and astonishingly relevant Word of God. This book links, in a most sane way, Bible answers and contemporary happenings throughout the world.

Billy Graham, at the climax of his New York crusade in September, 1991, having recently had lengthy conversations with world leaders such as Bush, Gorbachev, and Yeltsen and having been a close-up observer of the world-shaking events of 1991 (Desert Storm and the failed coup in Russia), said "About the coming of Armageddon . . . it seems to me that we are drawing close to that time."[1] He quoted from an article in *Time* magazine which stated:

> The future [now] suddenly looked problematic and dangerous. What of the 27,000 nuclear warheads deployed on missiles, bombers, submarines and at ammunition dumps across the old Union (USSR)? . . . It conjures up apocalyptic projections. Dick Elkus, an advisory board member of the Washington-based Center for Strategic and International Studies, predicted, "What has happened so far is a 6.0 earthquake on its way to becoming an 8.3—900 times greater." The Harriman Institute's Richard Ericson said, "we are facing what is perhaps the largest man-made disaster the world has ever seen."[2]

Harvard's B.F. Skinner, the Dean of Behaviorists, perhaps more than any other person in this half of the century, has dominated the field of psychology. He died shortly after Saddam Hussein's charge into Kuwait, but not without warning the world, from the platform of an American Psychological Association convention:

When I wrote *Beyond Freedom and Dignity* I was optimistic about the future. A decade ago there was hope, [but] today the world is fatally ill. . . . It is a very depressing way to end one's life. . . . The argument that we have always solved our problems in the past and shall, therefore, solve this one is like reassuring a dying man by pointing out that he has always recovered from his illness.

Skinner's demanding and distinctive question was: "Why are we not acting to save the world?" The real answer to Skinner's question is what Jerry Johnston is doing. God sent His Son into the world that the world through Him might be saved. Therefore only Jesus Christ can save the world (for which His imminent return is programmed). Jerry Johnston is out there, where the spiritual harvest is ripe, tracking down souls by the thousands and seeing them saved through repentance and faith in Jesus Christ as Lord.

—John Wesley White, D.Phil. (Oxford)
Associate Evangelist to Billy Graham
Toronto, Canada
September, 1991

1

I Will Come Again

◆ ═══════════════════════════ ◆

I had been gone from home for several days. After speaking at a conference in Lakeland, Florida, I dismounted the platform as the huge neon digital clock blared 12:01 P.M. My departure from the Tampa Airport was 1:05 P.M., at least an hour away. On top of it all, my rental car had to be returned. I also had luggage to check.

"Here we go again, Lord," I lamented to myself as my host shielded me from anyone wanting to stop me and rushed me to the waiting car. (I had done this O.J. Simpson dash hundreds of times before, and you would think I would have learned my lesson by now!)

To expedite my exit, my car had been moved curbside to the gargantuan 8500-seat sanctuary, and somehow I made it, thanks in large part to my favorite airline carrier.

Once I had settled into my seat and was airborne, I slipped into a reflective and contemplative mood. I reminded myself that I was bound for yet another city—Detroit—and wouldn't be home for days. As clear as if they were standing in the aisle, I pictured my eleven-year-old Danielle, ten-year-old Jeremy, six-year-old Jenilee, and my darling wife, Christie. And sitting there I actually began to cry. Quickly I shielded my face so the flight attendant and veteran businessman to my left wouldn't see me. Gazing out my oval window, the dismal gray sky seemed in perfect concert with the tears that streaked my face. I was so lonely for the four dearest friends I know. We five are a family, but first and foremost we are friends, real friends.

Earlier, on the way to the airport in the van, we made exciting plans for the first Friday night upon my return. Like a football team in a huddle, we stacked our hands on top of each other in agreement, anticipating our future joyous time together.

I had clearly told them I was going to return. And I told them when to expect my return. There was not even the slightest doubt in my mind that they were preparing for my return. I knew that the minute I walked off the plane, at the familiar Kansas City Airport, Christie would be there with upstretched arms. She would be dressed beautifully, with my favorite lipstick on, and would sparkle with the glamour that is unique to her.

The kids would board the bus two houses down on the morning of my return with an airlift to every step. They would be so much more confident. Their teachers wouldn't even have to be told; they would know that Mr. Johnston must be coming home today.

I would get ambushed with hugs when the bus dropped them off at 3:40 P.M. Instead of walking drearily the half-block, Danielle and Jeremy would run home. Danielle wouldn't even mind getting my slippers or starting my bathwater, my first stop upon every return. And no one would complain of Dad being a "newshound" for commandeering the TV to the CBS Evening News. The atmosphere of our family reunited at home would swallow me up and we would pillow our heads the first night as if there were not a care in the world.

Why would all this happen? Simply because I told my family I was going to return. The separation made them long for my return. They knew I would not lie to them. Never would it cross their minds that I would leave and never return, leaving them fearful to face the future alone. They would live every day, like I do, with joyful expectancy of our great reunion.

In the exact same way this serves as an illustration to us as Christians, and our soon-to-return Savior, Jesus Christ. Reflect for a moment on His promise, *"I will come again"* (John 14:3). This statement alone should be enough for us to anticipate His return. It is so simple and yet so profound: *I will come again.*

This changeless promise is not alone. In fact there are over 300 additional promises in the New Testament guaranteeing Christ's return. Jesus is indeed coming again.

I want to be like Danielle, Jeremy, Jenilee, and Christie— in a spiritual sense—and live every day preparing for His return. No attraction or pursuit of this world should supersede our keen interest in the return of Jesus Christ.

Of all the crowns promised to believers at the judgment seat of Christ, the crown of glory is reserved only for Christians who have His return in predominate focus: "When the Chief Shepherd appears, you will receive the unfading crown of glory" (1 Peter 5:4). Don't you want that crown?

In *The Last Days of Planet Earth* I have highlighted what I feel are the most urgent aspects of Christ's return. It is my prayer that God will use this to bring people to Christ. Furthermore, I hope that this will ignite the fuse in every Christian's heart to share His story with eagerness and enthusiasm.

Ever since the day as a burned-out drug-user when I turned to Christ I have received the ceaseless thrill of leading people to the same decision. For His own purposes

God has put me before a large number of young people internationally. As I survey the decadence of the young generation today, I am all the more convinced that Christ's coming must be near.

Lest I sound too negative, I am also seeing a receptivity to the gospel that is unprecedented. A strong demarcation is being drawn between those who are turning to Christ and those who are turning away from Him. As the prophet Joel has stated, "Rejoice, O sons of Zion, and be glad in the Lord your God, for He has given you the early rain for your vindication. And He has poured down for you the rain, the *early* and *latter* rain as before" (Joel 2:23).

Yes, I truly believe there will be a *latter* rain of God's Spirit, and that multitudes will find Christ. However, evil will continue to grow more widespread as we approach the second coming of Jesus Christ. The Bible paints a picture of widespread horror known as the tribulation period: Darkness and evil will abound on this planet; Satan's Antichrist will emerge; plagues and judgments will be unleashed upon this planet. To deny these realities one would have to rip entire sections out of the Bible, for the end-time scenario is presented with great clarity and stunning horror. Although Christ's light can penetrate anywhere, God has designated a time of great darkness to fall on planet Earth.

What is that light, and what is that darkness? Let's explore what the future holds.

2

A Futurist Prophesies What's Ahead

◆ ══════════════════ ◆

Your thoughts turned to what would take place in the future.

— Daniel 2:29

What does the future hold for planet Earth and its 5 billion inhabitants? A puzzling question indeed, and it is being answered in many ways. Spinning on its axis, earth is quickly populating with new minds who are seeking the answer to this quandary. Some, because of their impoverished state, don't care. The goal is simply to survive and at best to ease their suffering.

Yet earth is following a preplanned route much like the programmed computers of Spaceship Challenger. Together we will explore this odyssey—an adventure through the pages of this book that will leave you surprised and perhaps even stunned. More about these predicted steps later, but for a moment consider the challenge that our planet faces.

According to the Population Reference Bureau, the human growth rate is now three people per second, 180 per minute, 10,800 per hour, 259,200 per day, 1,814,400 per week, 94,348,800 per year!

What does the future hold for all these millions? When Jesus Christ was on earth nearly 2000 years ago, the population of the entire world was only 250 million, about 5 percent of the present-day figure. By 1650, nearly 17 centuries later, earth's inhabitants had doubled, to 500 million. Two hundred years after that we hit one billion, and in the last hundred years we have quintupled in size!

And this growth explosion is not over. Given the same calculations (including present-day birth- and death-rate variables), population experts think the growth will not slow down before earth's population has reached 10 billion or more! This meteoric boom is predicted to take place in well under 100 years.

A planet exploding with people means problems of every kind—pollution, congestion, disease, and much more. For instance, just in the United States (an industrialized nation), highway vehicle delay from 1985 to 2000 is expected to increase from 3 billion to 12 billion vehicle-hours annually, not to mention the increased number of traffic accidents caused by more people. According to the National Research Committee there are nearly 18 million crashes, 4 million injuries, and 45,000 fatalities on U.S. highways per year right now!

EXPLODING POPULATION

Let's look closer at what all of this means. Noted population researchers Paul and Anne Ehrlich, professors at Stanford University and coauthors of the 1990 Simon and Schuster book *The Population Explosion*, sketch the international burgeoning population trends and the automatic threat imposed.

Their insistence is that we must put the brakes on the ever-increasing number of humans birthing into an already depleted, troubled world. They have an action plan which includes writing the Pope to protest his anticontraceptive Catholic position.

Aided by numerous world-watching organizations, the Ehrlichs reveal the ominous threats posed for the future of planet Earth. Global warming, acid rain, depletion of the ozone layer, vulnerability to epidemics, and exhaustion of soils and groundwater are all storm clouds on man's future horizon, and are all clearly population-linked.

Consider the picture they paint in *The Population Explosion* of earth pregnant with people:

> With no change in family size (and a small reduction in immigration), the Census Bureau projects that our [U.S.] population will stop growing and start shrinking gradually around 2040, when there will be over 300 million of us (p. 228).

> There are about a billion Moslems in the world.... With an average completed family size of about six children, Moslems are reproducing faster than any other major religious group, despite death rates of almost 14 per 1000 and tragically high infant mortality rates that reach about 150 per 1000 live births in West Africa (p. 212).

> With the present unequal distribution of food, a billion or so people are, if anything, too well fed. Most of them, of course, are in rich countries. About a third of the world's grain harvest is fed to livestock so that the diets of the well-to-do can be enriched with meat, eggs, and dairy products. Perhaps 3 billion other people get enough to eat, although meat may not often grace their dinner tables. Nearly a billion of the world's poorest people, mostly in poor countries, are

hungry. An estimated 950 million people were getting deficient diets in 1988—roughly one out of three people living in developing nations outside China. About two out of five of those (almost 400 million people) were so undernourished that their health was threatened or their growth was stunted (p. 67).

Suppose . . . that China's population remained at 1.1 billion . . . demographers project it to rise at least to 1.4 or 1.5 billion, and some Chinese experts claim it has already exceeded 1.2 billion (p. 113).

In 2000, there are projected to be twenty cities of more than 10 million [people], seventeen of them in developing nations. Overall, about half of humanity will be living in cities before 2010, more than three billion people (p. 153).

If the ability of the AIDS virus to grow in the cells of the skin or the membranes of the mouth, the lungs, or the intestines were increased, the virus might be spread by casual contact, by inhalation, or through eating contaminated food.

Nobel laureate Joshua Lederberg is worried that a relatively minor mutation could lead to the virus infecting a type of white blood cell commonly present in the lungs. If so, it might be transmissible through coughs (p. 148).

Indeed, William McNeill has argued that epidemics have played a key role in the rise and fall of many civilizations (p. 140).

And all of this is only the hem of the garment. The Ehlrichs say we are already in deep trouble. Somehow this speeding global train must be slowed down.

What does the future hold? The very word "future" is a teasing concept. One of the most important aspects of life for determining what is going to happen in the activities of life is to study the thoughts, projections, and plans of the futurists.

This is a group of secular intellectuals who are regarded as experts in their respective field. They represent the academic, scientific, and technical areas of life. They are the drivers of world opinion. By nature, they are internationalists.

THE THREE PARTS OF LIFE

It would be of ostrich intelligence to not know the trends of the future, and to not be in contact with happenings of those trends as they occur. There are actually only three parts of life: the past, the present, and the future. History records the past. For the secular world, history is a combination of facts and conjecture as viewed and interpreted by the historian making the reporting.

The present is life as it exists now. It must be viewed as reality.

The future is an interpretation by whoever is the interpreter. It must of necessity be based on many considerations and finally projected as a future happening.

Forecasts represent a tremendous range of visions for the future, including such things as living computers, robot servants, genetically engineered food, space colonies, and high-tech medical miracles. The visions are of promises of happiness and fears of doom. They seem to contradict each other, but this is typical of the futurists' predictions.

One of the futurists' concerns is that of the invasion of one's personal privacy as computer databases grow. Projected already are computers that will store information on virtually every aspect of our lives—the videos we rent, the various causes we contribute to, the answers we give to personal opinion and research polls on everything from reproductive issues to drug abuse, and the financial applications we make for loans. The computer information base being collected on individuals is becoming priceless and powerful, for it will be capable of presenting a psychological profile on a person in virtually every area of his or her life.

Changes are inevitable, and according to some experts they may be nearly immediate because of rapidly developing technological and social advances. For example, the rapid social progress of Eastern Europe shows that the long-term prospects of millions of people can be realized in just a matter of days.

In the ensuing chapters I will address specifically my belief in the future. However, first come with me and catch a glimpse of the international futurists and their report of present and future trends.

Envisioning the Fan of the Futures

The "greenhouse effect," a potential global environmental crisis, will generate problems that national and world leaders will be forced to respond to. One of the worst examples of a greenhouse gas effect is the infamous burning of the Kuwaiti oil wells by Iraq's Saddam Hussein. Mount St. Helens' volcanic ash explosion and the Chernobyl nuclear accident are other classic cases.

An 80 percent increase in carbon emissions is expected in the next 20 years unless policies are developed to harness this threat to the environment.

Senior Denmark scientist Sigurd O. Nielson comments on the fan of the futures.

One of the operational definitions of futures research can be stated as "mapping the present in order to decide and act on the future." Futures research directs those in management positions to focus critically on the fan of anticipated futures.

Futurists' concept of the future is that of a "fan" of anticipated futures that is subject to continuing revision as more knowledge becomes available. Decisions come in pairs: The choice of a preferred future is always coupled with the fan of futures that reflects the full spectrum of premises on which the decision is made.

If the choice is made, for instance, to wait 10 years or more for definite research results on the greenhouse effect before making decisions on the allowed rate that greenhouse gases may be released into the atmosphere, there is a risk that the self-regulatory climatic system of the earth could, in the meantime, be irreversibly overwhelmed, with consequent catastrophic, global disturbances.[1]

TIME TRAVEL: A GUIDE TO JOURNEYS IN THE FOURTH DIMENSION

At present man can easily travel around the world by jet. In eight hours you can fly from Chicago to Frankfurt or Honolulu. Another eight hours will take you half the world farther. In another eight hours you can stretch almost around the globe.

The supersonic Concorde which takes off from Washington or New York can whip you to London in a little over two hours. Defying the speed of sound, it is one of the grand phenomena of commercial travel. However, all of this is archaic compared to what is ahead.

Popular Science magazine (May 1991) reports on preliminary sketches by Airbus Industries of a new super-aircraft. Renovated with a new flattened fuselage design, the airplane could accommodate 600 passengers and fly a minimum of 8000 miles without refueling. If plans are confirmed, expect the aircraft in 2003.

Crossing the Atlantic in a tunnel in a single hour or traveling from New York to Los Angeles in 30 minutes, hypersonic trains may one day exceed any calculation of time travel today. These trains, according to some experts, would fly in the vacuum created by pumping the air out of a long-distance transit tube.

John W. Macvey, a fellow of the Royal Astronomical Society and owner of his own observatory, has his own speculation of future travel.

> Access to the future might be obtained through relativistic travel, or time dilation, which would require interstellar travel near the velocity of light. The consequence of velocities approaching that of light is the slowing down of time. Thus a theoretical vessel traveling at a slight fraction less than light velocity could make a 4.5-million-light-year round-trip journey to the Great Galaxy in Andromeda in just 55 years, returning to Earth 4.7 million years in the future.[2]

Future travel will not only take us transcontinentally or internationally in record speed, but out of our atmosphere in space exploration.

TOWARD A MORALITY OF DYING

Dr. Robert M. Veatch, professor of medical ethics at Georgetown University, has written two books on death and dying and hinted at the slow-but-sure biological revolution that is taking place.

In his recent *Death and Dying and the Biological Revolution*, Dr. Veatch attempts to divide and define death as either irreversible cessation of all the functions of the brain or as simple loss of higher brain capabilities.

> Measuring "signs of life" is no longer simple, thanks to the development of organ-transplant techniques and such devices as the mechanical respirator and the artificial heart. As Veatch points out, "It is not the heart and lungs as such that are essentially significant but rather the vital functions . . . associated with these organs." In other words, a living body must have some means of circulating blood and oxygen. "If modern technology produced an efficient, compact heart-lung machine capable of being carried on the back or in the pocket, people using such devices would not be considered dead, even though both heart and lungs were permanently non-functioning."
>
> For the present, the brain remains one organ that most social and legal authorities can agree is essential to human life. But even "brain death" definitions may not always be final. To quote Veatch: "An 'artificial brain' is not possible at present, but a walking, thinking individual who had one would certainly be considered living."[3]

It is indeed scary to think of future medical attempts and capabilities which acknowledge neither God nor man as His created being. We hear now of people being abducted and their vital organs surgically removed to be sold on the black market for diseased individuals whose only hope for life requires such organs. There have been documented cases of this in New York and other major cities. The dignity of each individual life will be lost by people desperately trying to survive as death and disease increase.

Increasingly and undenyingly we are rapidly moving to a global community, or to use President Bush's expression, the New World Order. Via the computer, academicians and practitioners from virtually every field interested in the use of intuition and data will be linked together.

Weston H. Agor, professor of public administration at the University of Texas at El Paso, remarks that the use of intuition is increasingly studied as a potential tool for improving thinking, learning, and decision-making processes.

THE WORK/LIFE DICHOTOMY

Psychologist Martin Morf in his 1989 book says there are deeper problems than the economic worries brought on by noncompetitiveness and decline in worker productivity.

> He asserts that the severe productivity problems being experienced in the United States and other Western nations are the result of a crippling dichotomy between work life and home life. Morf examines what he views as a complex relationship between society, culture, and work. What is needed is an interactive view of the relationship between work and life and between job and worker. While this perspective is often demonstrated by Japanese firms, it is rare in U.S. companies. He adds that many of the actions that need to be taken are, while important, relatively small. "Small changes in our behavior and attitudes may produce meaningful effects in the course of time."[4]

GENETIC ENGINEERING

Genetic engineering may produce biological weapons of the future that will be even more deadly than existing weapons. A strain of "super-bacteria" containing several different toxins could result in diseases beyond the capability of coping with them by medical treatment. The inevitable result could be physical complications of pandemic proportions.

We don't know all that lies ahead, but the first test-tube baby is now a young infant. Artificial insemination is widely practiced. The question is: Will we move toward genetic selection of birth, and of particular features of a desired child? Black-market birthing is already widespread in different parts of the world. Where will it all lead?

HEALTH-CARE RENOVATION

Health-care costs have already attained a level that 40 million Americans are not covered by insurance. United Way Strategic Institute reports that health-care costs in the United States will triple between 1987 and 2000. The United States currently spends about 1.5 billion dollars *a day* on health care. Ordinary medicines in America cost more than anywhere else in the civilized world. Over 500 billion dollars are spent each year on health care, more than 11 percent of the Gross National Product. One night in a United States hospital room can cost more than reserving a suite in a world-class hotel.

As victims of AIDS grow, needing extensive health care, experts contend that there is a potential medical holocaust ahead. At least a third of U.S. teenagers are sexually active by age 15. Health-care experts suggest that teenagers will be ravaged by the AIDS virus in the next several years. The aging of America represents new challenges medically.

> The continuing aging of the workforce will create problems and opportunities. The aging of the baby-boom generation (people born between 1946 and 1964) is raising the median age of the U.S. population. The median age, about 33 in 1990, will be 36 by the year 2000. By 2010, one quarter of the U.S. population will be at least 55, and one in seven Americans will be at least 65. More than 31 million Americans—12.4 percent of the nation's population—are estimated to be 65 or older. By 2020, when baby boomers reach 65, old people will be 20 percent of the U.S. population. At that time there will be at least 7 million Americans over age 85.[5]

Obviously there has to be a medical overhaul. What medical wizardry lies ahead? Blind people may have their sight restored by transplanting the light-sensitive cells of the eyes. Experts have already successfully transplanted photoreceptor tissue into the eyes of rats.

Some futurists even prophesy that "microrobots may perform surgery from inside the patient's body. After being swallowed by the patient, a microrobot would be guided by a human surgeon 'seeing' the inside of the patient through a combination of computer imaging and 3-D simulation."[6]

AND MUCH MORE...

I have mentioned only a few of the future predictions of life, whether promising or menacing, but there is much more on the agenda—like the dramatic change of the family unit. In 1987, of the 50.3 million employed women, 59.2 percent were married. The rise in single parents, blended families, and homosexual families will present urgent challenges.

Underground cities are planned. In Japan, some of the largest construction companies have adopted rough sketches of such cities. Reduction of urban crowding, protection against earthquakes, and an increase in energy efficiency are just a few of the plus points of the underground cities.

Even "living computers" may be possible in the next ten years. Researchers have genetically engineered protein molecules that collectively act as transistors. Future biochips, or living computers, will be smaller and faster than semiconductors and will generate less heat. With specialized functions such as the sense of smell, biochips could identify poisonous fumes in a factory and order the equipment to shut down.

Some are predicting that multipurpose robot servants will be developed in the next century to replace virtually the entire workforce. The list and features of each category of futurism is almost endless.

GOD'S PROPHETIC PLAN

In spite of man's predictions and blueprint for the future, God has a divine plan of His own. The Holy Scriptures predict very clearly that Jesus Christ is going to return to this planet. The return of Christ will bring about the end of this present world as we know it. Pivotally, it will usher in a new era of man far beyond anything I have just detailed.

Daniel asked the critical question, "How long will it be until the end of these wonders?" (Daniel 12:6). And the angel answered, "Go your way, Daniel, for these words are concealed and sealed up until the end time. Many will be purged, purified, and refined . . . but those who have insight will understand" (Daniel 12:9,10).

God has spoken extensively through His prophets for hundreds of years regarding the end time. The prophets many times did not understand their own prophecies. However, for the people living in the end times God promises insight if we will only search the Scriptures. The words that were concealed for generations are now blazingly lucid and bright to those who live in this time age.

Believe the Bible literally. Though some things will continue to be concealed, Paul challenges us as Christians to be informed and *ready*! "But you, brethren, are not in darkness, that the day should overtake you like a thief; for you are all sons of light and sons of day. We are not of night nor of darkness, so then let us not sleep as others do, but let us be alert and sober. For those who sleep do their sleeping at night, and those who get drunk get drunk at night. But since we are of the day, let us be sober, having put on the breastplate of faith and love, and as a helmet the hope of salvation. For God has not destined us for wrath, but for obtaining salvation through our Lord Jesus Christ" (1 Thessalonians 5:4-9).

Jesus is coming. When? "Of that day and hour no one knows, not even the angels of heaven, nor the Son, but the Father alone" (Matthew 24:36).

That hour is coming. As you read each chapter of this book, you will be convinced that the hour of His return is very soon. Let's embark on our journey together.

3

Irrefutable Proofs of Christ's Return

✦ ============================== ✦

In the last days mockers will come with their mocking, following after their own lust, and saying, "Where is the promise of His coming? For ever since the fathers fell asleep, all continues just as it was from the beginning of creation.

—2 Peter 3:3,4

The most amazing aspect of the Bible is that it not only describes the origin of man but intricately describes the final stages of planet Earth and its inhabitants. This broad area of study is known theologically under the title "eschatology." Eschatology is simply the final outcome of the present world. God has a sovereign plan to bring the world and its inhabitants to a great finale.

The Bible, made up of 66 books (39 in the Old Testament and 27 in the New Testament), has many irrefutable proofs that Jesus Christ is going to return to planet Earth. As we have seen, man has many predictions of what the future holds. Almost everyone agrees that the world as we know it will not last forever. Even with all the academic and intellectual advances, man still lives approximately 70 to 80 years.

Perhaps the most basic question which plagues every thinking person is what lies ahead.

The Bible predicts irrefutably that Christ is going to
return. However, before His actual return to planet Earth
an ominous scenario of devastating proportions will grip
this planet. How can we know? Is it possible to be absolutely
certain? What are these irrefutable proofs?

PROOF 1:
THE ACCURACY OF
BIBLICAL PREDICTIONS

Prophecy occupies about one-fifth of the entire Bible.
Incredibly, the second coming of Christ takes up about one-
third of all of biblical prophecy. In the Old Testament there
are over 660 general prophecies, and at least 330 of these
are concerning Jesus Christ.

Of these 330 prophecies strictly applying to Jesus Christ,
over 100 were fulfilled in His first coming. This leaves over
200 prophecies which will be fulfilled in the finest detail in
Christ's second coming.

The Old Testament contains at least 46 men who were
known as "prophets." These men of faith, under the inspiration of God, foretold the future. Many of their predictions
are included in the Bible, and several comprise entire books
(Isaiah, Jeremiah, Ezekiel, Daniel, Joel, Zechariah, etc.).
Although they lived in past centuries and cultures, their
inspired words were divinely designed to predict future
events in detail. Less than ten of the Old Testament prophets
prophesied events in Jesus Christ's first coming. Astound-
ingly, at least 35 of them predicted events in the *second*
coming of Christ! One Bible teacher estimates that there
are a total of 1520 Old Testament passages concerning

Jesus' second coming alone! The New Testament's 27 books contain 7959 individual verses. Over 300 passages refer clearly to the second coming of Christ.

For every time the Bible mentions the first coming of Christ, there are 20 references to His second coming! Even Jesus Christ Himself referred to His return 21 times. Over 50 verses in the New Testament caution us to be ready for Christ's return.

H. Harold Hartzler, of the American Scientific Affiliation, writes in the foreword of Peter Stoner's book, "The manuscript for *Science Speaks* has been carefully reviewed by a committee of the American Scientific Affiliation and by the Executive Council of the same group and has found, in general, to be dependable and accurate in regard to the scientific material presented. The mathematical analysis included is based upon principles of probability which are thoroughly sound, and Professor Stoner has applied these principles in a proper and convincing way."

The following probabilities are taken from Peter Stoner in *Science Speaks* (Moody Press, 1963) to show that coincidence is ruled out by the science of probability. Stoner says that by using the modern science of probability in reference to eight prophecies, "we find that the chance that any man might have lived down to the present time and fulfilled all eight prophecies is 1 in 10^{17}." That would be 1 in 100,000,000,000,000,000. In order to help us comprehend this staggering probability, Stoner illustrates it by supposing that 'we take 10^{17} silver dollars and lay them on the face of Texas. They will cover all of the state two feet deep. Now mark one of these silver dollars and stir the whole mass thoroughly, all over the state. Blindfold a man and tell him that he can travel as far as he wishes, but he must pick up one silver dollar and say that it is the right one. What chance would he have of getting the right one? Just the same chance that the prophets would have had of writing these eight prophecies and having them all come true in any one man, from their day to the present time, providing they wrote them in their own wisdom.[1]

These are probabilities for just *eight* prophecies, and there are *hundreds* in the Bible that have been minutely fulfilled.

The Bible is no ordinary book. That is why every single year it is the leading bestseller of all books in print. The Bible was verbally inspired by God and forms the basis for our faith and spiritual practice. The Scriptures give heavy emphasis to the second coming of Jesus Christ.

We should not pass over lightly the authority of the inspiration of Scripture. Our belief in the second coming is reinforced when we understand the accuracy of Scripture's prophetic Word.

Dr. Henry Morris, eminent apologist for the Christian faith, outlines the authority, infallibility, and inspiration of the Bible in five specific areas.

◆ *Unity in diversity.* Consisting of 66 separate books written by about 40 different authors over a span of at least 2000 years...[the Bible] presents a marvelous unity. There is nothing remotely comparable to [the Bible] among all the millions of books written by man.

◆ *Fulfilled prophecy.* There are hundreds of prophecies recorded in Scripture which have been meticulously fulfilled, often hundreds of years later. This is a unique characteristic of the Bible not found in the Vedas or the Koran or any of the other "scriptures" of mankind.

◆ *Accuracy.* [The Bible] proved accurate in its very frequent references to matters of history and principles of natural science. It is ... true that archaeological and historical research has confirmed the Biblical references in hundreds of instances and that scores of now-known facts of science were written in the Bible long before men recognized them in nature.

◆ *Unique preservation.* No other book has ever been the object of such antagonism ... kings and priests have tried desperately to destroy it and unbelieving intellectuals to ridicule and refute it. Untold numbers of copies have been burned and mutilated and hosts of its advocates persecuted and killed. But it has only multiplied the more and today is read and believed by more people in more nations and languages than ever before, continually remaining for centuries the world's best seller.

◆ *Claims of its writers.* Although other writers such as Mohammed have claimed divine inspiration for their writings, the frequency and variety of such assertions are unique to the Bible.

In the Old Testament, the writers with great frequency claim to be recording the very words of the Lord.

Books of Moses: 680 claims of inspiration

Prophetical Books: 1307 claims of inspiration

Historical Books: 418 claims of inspiration

Poetical Books: 195 claims of inspiration

Entire Old Testament: 2600 claims of inspiration.[2]

Too often we as Christians don't understand that we carry and read a divinely inspired Book. Every prophecy will be fulfilled with precision. Jesus said, "Heaven and earth will pass away, but My words shall not pass away" (Matthew 24:35). It would be easier for earth to disintegrate than for God's Word to go unfulfilled.

> The written records of Christian origins are in this respect available in far greater variety and antiquity than are those of any other personages or happenings in the whole history of the world prior to the invention of printing! No one, for example, ever doubts for an instant that a man named Julius Caesar once ruled as Emperor of Rome. But the manuscript evidence for the New Testament events is incomparably superior to that for the existence of Caesar.
>
> The manuscript copies of the New Testament or portions thereof that have actually been preserved to the present day are amazingly numerous. Some of these are on papyrus fragments that were copied as early as the middle of the second century. Altogether there are probably available today over 5000 manuscript copies of portions of the New Testament in Greek and at least 15,000 more in other languages. Nothing remotely comparable to this abundance exists for any other ancient writing.
>
> Although there are many individual differences found in the New Testament text as preserved in these 20,000 manuscripts, the very number of them provides

a powerful means of checking and tracing the origin of the variant readings and thus of ascertaining the original text. Furthermore, the discrepancies, whether caused by careless copying or by deliberate alterations, are in almost all cases quite trivial, affecting no important fact or doctrine.[3]

If the Bible predicts the second coming of Christ, and it does, you can be guaranteed that it will come to pass! God's Word has proved itself over time and time again. Consider the following.

At one time science said the earth was flat. From the beginning God's Word said the earth is a sphere; science now concurs (Isaiah 40:22).

At one time science said every star was identical. From the beginning God's Word said they were different; science now concurs (1 Corinthians 15:41).

At one time science said winds blows straight. From the beginning God's Word said winds blow in cyclones; science now concurs (Ecclesiastes 1:6).

At one time science said sick people must be bled. From the beginning God's Word said blood is a source of life and healing; science now concurs (Leviticus 17:11).

At one time science said light is fixed in place. From the beginning God's Word said light is in motion; science now concurs (Job 38:19,20).

Every prophecy of the Bible will be fulfilled!

PROOF 2:
FIRST-COMING
PROPHECIES FULFILLED

The same Bible which predicts the second coming of Jesus Christ also foretold of the *first* coming of the Messiah. How invigorating it is to realize how specific God was concerning the prophetic prediction of Jesus' first coming to earth!

In the Old Testament God promised a Messiah. God also promised that when the Messiah came He would do certain things and be treated in a specific way. Every one of those prophecies was fulfilled in the finest detail.

Remember, of the 330 Old Testament prophecies concerning the Messiah (Jesus), over 100 were fulfilled in Christ's first coming to the earth. Each first-coming promise reminds us of the guarantee of Christ's second coming. Note these fulfilled prophecies in your Bible.

1. *God said the Messiah would be born of a virgin.* "Therefore the Lord Himself will give you a sign: Behold, a virgin will be with child and bear a son, and she will call His name Immanuel" (Isaiah 7:14). This unique promise was made at least 700 years before the birth of Christ! Now listen to Matthew 1:23: "Behold, the virgin shall be with child, and shall bear a Son, and they shall call His name Immanuel, which translated means 'God with us.'"

2. *God said the Messiah would be born in Bethlehem.* "But as for you, Bethlehem Ephrathah.... from you One will go forth for Me to be ruler in Israel" (Micah 5:2). The mention of the very city of the Messiah's birth was given by the prophet 700 years before

Jesus was born in a manger in Bethlehem. The fulfillment is found in Matthew 2:1: "Now after Jesus was born in Bethlehem of Judea in the days of Herod the king, behold, magi from the east arrived in Jerusalem."

3. *God said the Messiah would be incarnate God.* "A child will be born to us, a son will be given to us... and His name will be called Wonderful, Counselor, Mighty God, Eternal Father, Prince of Peace" (Isaiah 9:6). Here again, this prophetic word was given 750 years before the birth of Christ. Note Matthew 1:23: "...and shall bear a Son, and they shall call His name Immanuel, which translated means 'God with us.'" Jesus Christ was God made evident in the form of a man. As a sinless God-man He became our deliverer.

4. *God said that one of Jesus' close friends would betray Him.* "Even my close friend, in whom I trusted, who ate my bread, has lifted up his heel against me" (Psalm 41:9). It was Judas who, after breaking bread with Jesus at our Lord's last supper, went out and betrayed Him. "Then one of the twelve, named Judas Iscariot, went to the chief priests and said, 'What are you willing to give me to deliver Him up to you?' And they weighed out to him thirty pieces of silver" (Matthew 26:14,15).

5. *God said the Messiah would be betrayed for thirty pieces of silver.* "I said to them, 'If it is good in your sight, give me my wages; but if not, never mind!' So they weighed out thirty shekels of silver as my wages" (Zechariah 11:12). The prophet Zechariah lived in the fifth century B.C.! It is stunning to read Matthew

26:15 knowing that the two verses were separated in time by hundreds of years!

6. *God said the Messiah would be forsaken by even His apostles.* " 'Awake, O sword, against My Shepherd, and against the man, My Associate,' declares the Lord of hosts. 'Strike the Shepherd that the sheep may be scattered; and I will turn My hand against the little ones' " (Zechariah 13:7). One of the saddest verses in the Bible must be Matthew 26:56: "Then all the disciples left Him and fled."

7. *God said the Messiah would enter Jerusalem on the seat of a donkey.* "Rejoice greatly, O daughter of Zion! Shout in triumph, O daughter of Jerusalem! Behold, your king is coming to you; He is just and endowed with salvation, humble and mounted on a donkey, even on a colt, the foal of donkey" (Zechariah 9:9). Here is the New Testament counterpart: "When they had approached Jerusalem and had come to Bethphage, to the Mount of Olives, then Jesus sent two disciples, saying to them, 'Go into the village opposite you, and immediately you will find a donkey tied there and a colt with her; untie them and bring them to Me. And if anyone says something to you, you shall say, The Lord has need of them, and immediately he will send them' " (Matthew 21:1-3).

8. *God said the money received by betraying the Messiah would be used to buy a potter's field.* "Then the Lord said to me, 'Throw it to the potter, that magnificent price at which I was valued by them.' So I took the thirty shekels of silver and threw them to the potter in the house of the Lord" (Zechariah 11:13). After

committing suicide, Judas' treasonous money was used to buy a potter's field: "And they counseled together and with the money bought the Potter's Field as a burial place for strangers. For this reason that field has been called the Field of Blood to this day" (Matthew 27:7,8).

9. *God said the Messiah would suffer extreme physical torture.* "I gave My back to those who strike Me, and My cheeks to those who pluck out the beard; I did not cover My face from humiliation and spitting" (Isaiah 50:6). Imagine the scene: This was God in human flesh that men were abusing. "And they spat on Him, and took the reed and began to beat Him on the head. And after they had mocked Him, they took His robe off and put His garments on Him, and led Him away to crucify Him" (Matthew 27:30,31).

10. *God said the Messiah would be crucified.* An unknown form of capital punishment death in David's day, crucifixion for Jesus was prophesied at least 400 years before the Romans invented this hideous form of death. "But I am a worm, and not a man, a reproach of men, and despised by the people" (Psalm 22:6). Notice verse 14: "I am poured out like water, and all my bones are out of joint; my heart is like wax; it is melted within me." Now notice verse 16: "For dogs have surrounded me; a band of evildoers has encompassed me; they *pierced my hands and my feet.*" The prophet Zechariah meticulously signals the piercing of Christ's hand: "They will look on Me *whom they have pierced*" (Zechariah 12:10). The New Testament responds: "And when they had crucified Him,

they divided up His garments among themselves, casting lots" (Matthew 27:35).

11. *God said they would attempt to medicate the Messiah while He was dying.* In Psalm 69:21 David says, "They also gave me gall for my food, and for my thirst they gave me vinegar to drink." The fulfillment is clear in Matthew 27:34: "They gave Him wine to drink mingled with gall; and after tasting it, He was unwilling to drink."

12. *God said that not one of the Messiah's bones would be broken.* "He keeps all his bones; not one of them is broken" (Psalm 34:20). John's narrative confirms this: "The soldiers therefore came, and broke the legs of the first man, and of the other man who was crucified with Him; but coming to Jesus, when they saw that He was already dead, they *did not* break His legs" (John 19:32,33).

These are just 12 of over 100 Old Testament Bible predictions regarding the first coming of Christ that were literally and specifically fulfilled. Their literal fulfillment reminds us that all of the 200-plus Old Testament predictions concerning Christ's second coming will unquestionably come to pass. I have not taken the time to relate the significant messianic chapter of Isaiah 53, but take a moment and read it. Without a doubt it is a picture of Jesus on the cross. And this chapter is quoted in at least six different places in the New Testament.

Proof 3: The Continuation of the Church

The continuation of the church demands the return of the Lord Jesus Christ. Many Christians are unaware of what the term "church" means as it appears in Scripture. When we speak of the subject of the church we *are not* talking about buildings in which Christians meet. Those are simply buildings, regardless of how gothic or sanctimonious they may appear. And the biblical term "church" has no correlation whatsoever to any particular denomination. Denominations are of man, while the church was born of God. In heaven the only name that will be known is *Christian*, not Baptist, Catholic, Methodist, or Nazarene.

What or who then is the church? The words "church" or "churches" are used 114 times in the New Testament. The Greek word for church is *ekklesia*, meaning "assembly" or "ones called out from the mass of humanity." It is derived from two Greek words: *ek*, meaning "from" or "out of," and *kaleo*, meaning to "call." Eighty times the term "church" appears in the New Testament in the singular tense. Thirty-four times the term "church" appears in the plural. *Ekklesia* is also translated "assembly" in the New Testament.

The church was founded nearly 2000 years ago. On the Jewish Day of Pentecost there were probably over a million people in Jerusalem. The apostles and followers of Jesus Christ were at His command in the same city waiting on God in prayer for the fullness of the Holy Spirit and their commissioning. Jesus had consoled them by saying, "When I leave you, I will send the Comforter, the Holy Spirit; He will be in you."

Five times John spoke of this Comforter (John 14:16,26; 15:26; 16:7,13) by using a term that no other New Testament writer employed: *parakletos*. This word is a combination of two Greek words. The first half, *para*, means "alongside of." The second half, *kaleo*, means "to call." These two combined words, *parakletos*, give us the term "paraclete," which means "one called alongside." The Holy

Spirit is called alongside of every Christian to comfort, but more directly to help. What a beautiful thought!

Acts chapter 2 records the awesome power and result when the Holy Spirit came to inaugurate the church: After Peter's Spirit-endued message 3000 people accepted Christ! What a first day to have! The church born at Pentecost will be completed on earth at the *rapture*.

Most societies and organizations die when their founders do, although some live the second generation. Very few last two centuries. But the church, founded by Jesus Christ, nearly two millennia later is strong and burgeoning worldwide. In China and the Soviet Union the church is growing phenomenally. Romania, so oppressed for years by a godless dictator, is in the midst of one of the greatest revival of all times. Africa's churches are booming. And at least four of the very largest churches of the world are found in Korea, one of which boasts over 500,000 members!

Here in the United States the term "megachurch" is becoming commonplace. Building programs for church facilities of over 20-million dollars are quite common. After preaching in over a thousand churches in North America, I can attest that although every church needs revival as well as greater purity, passion, and zeal, nevertheless the church is very much alive. Hundreds of U.S. churches seat 1000 or more. Many seat 2500, and scores seat 5000 or more. John N. Vaughan, Church Growth expert, reports that 43 Protestant congregations in the U.S. claim 5000 or more Sunday worshipers. All of these churches are made up of born-again people of all races and socioeconomic classes who know Jesus Christ.

Jesus Christ is going to return for His church. In the Bible the church is described as a bride (2 Corinthians 11:2). Jesus is the Bridegroom. The parable that Jesus used in

Matthew 25 illustrates His strong love for the church: He is homesick to receive us back to Himself.

Christian stalwart John Walvoord points out that the wedding customs of the Oriental world had three aspects: the legal side (dowry paid), the betrothal (gifts given), and (a year later) the actual wedding ceremony.

When Jesus Christ comes for the church we will enter the third phase—a great ceremony, the marriage supper of the Lamb! What a celebration that will be! When you accepted Christ you were legally married to Jesus. And He paid a heavy dowry (price) for each one of us. Soon we are to be reunited.

The symbol of our marriage to Christ is exquisitely set forth in Ephesians 5, a reminder to me of how I am to love my wife, Christie. God says, "Husbands, love your wives, just as Christ also loved the church and gave Himself up for her, that He might sanctify her, having cleansed her by the washing of water with the word, that He might present to Himself the church in all her glory, having no spot or wrinkle or any such thing, but that she should be holy and blameless" (Ephesians 5:25-27).

Christ is going to return for His church—that's you and me!

PROOF 4:
THE PROMISE OF JESUS CHRIST

During his three-year earthly ministry Jesus repeatedly stressed that He was going to return to the earth. He gave a serious warning to be ready. In fact, the implied thought is that man will not be ready, not be looking for His return.

I have often wondered if this meant that Christ would

come while people were sleeping, or during an international event which will capture the masses' mind and attention. We don't know. But it was Jesus who spoke the
following words:

> You will be hearing of wars and rumors of wars; see
> that you are not frightened, for those things must take
> place, but that is not yet the end (Matthew 24:6).

> Then there will be a great tribulation, such as has
> not occurred since the beginning of the world until
> now, nor ever shall (Matthew 24:21).

> Just as the lightning comes from the east and flashes
> even to the west, so shall the coming of the Son of Man
> be (Matthew 24:27).

> Then the sign of the Son of Man will appear in the
> sky, and then all the tribes of the earth will mourn, and
> they will see the Son of Man coming on the clouds of
> the sky with power and great glory (Matthew 24:30).

> Of that day and hour no one knows, not even the
> angels of heaven, nor the Son, but the Father alone
> (Matthew 24:36).

> Be on the alert, for you do not know which day your
> Lord is coming. But be sure of this, that if the head of
> the house had known at what time of the night the
> thief was coming, he would have been on the alert and
> would not have allowed his house to be broken into.
> For this reason you be ready too; for the Son of Man is
> coming at an hour when you do not think He will
> (Matthew 24:42-44).

> When the Son of Man comes in His glory, and all the
> angels with Him, then He will sit on His glorious

throne. And all the nations will be gathered before Him; and He will separate them from one another, as the shepherd separates the sheep from the goats (Matthew 25:31,32).

Jesus said to him, "You have said it yourself; nevertheless I tell you, hereafter you shall see the Son of Man sitting at the right hand of Power, and coming on the clouds of heaven" (Matthew 26:64).

Jesus Christ promised His return. There was a day when He was humiliated, spit upon, and crucified, but that day is over. The resurrection of Christ reminds us that Jesus is going to return as King and Prince of all. In that day every knee will bow to Him. If these multiple promises of Christ are not fulfilled, then the Bible and the Christian faith would be invalid. But they are true; they will be fulfilled, down to the smallest detail: "Truly I say to you, until heaven and earth pass away, not the smallest letter or stroke shall pass away from the Law, until all is accomplished" (Matthew 5:18).

PROOF 5:
THE REORGANIZATION OF
THE NATION OF ISRAEL

Without a doubt this is the most stunning prophetic reality which points inexplicably to the return of Jesus Christ. The Bible teaches that God is sovereign. God is in total control; He rules in the affairs of man. From a human perspective, we say that a president is appointed by the will of the masses. However, God's Word makes it clear that it is actually the Lord who sets one man up and puts another down: "He it is who reduces rulers to nothing, who makes the judges of the earth meaningless" (Isaiah 40:23). This biblical principle also applies with the nations.

> Behold, the nations are like a drop from a bucket, and are regarded as a speck of dust on the scales (Isaiah 40:15).

> That the Most High is ruler over the realm of mankind, and bestows it on whom He wishes, and sets over it the lowliest of men (Daniel 4:17).

As God raised up a hardened, unbelieving Pharaoh for His eternal purpose, so God predicts the doom or blessing of the various nations of the world according to His plan.

In the plan of God, the Jewish nation was selected as the apple of God's eye. The covenant, which began with the believing patriarch Abraham approximately 4000 years ago, is still certain today. God said to Abraham, "I will make you a great nation, and I will bless you and make your name great; and so you shall be a blessing" (Genesis 12:2).

From this microscopic beginning the nation of Israel flourished under the reign of David, and also his son, Solomon. The Queen of Sheba, after surveying Israel in Solomon's day, said, "The half has never been told."

The Bible was written almost entirely by Jews. Jesus Himself was a Jew. God promised the nation of Israel blessings, health, and prosperity if they would obey Him.

God also promised that they would be scattered if they disobeyed Him and followed the customs of their neighboring pagan nations. Unlike other historic nations driven from their homeland, Israel would be temporarily dispersed but not terminated due to disobedience. "Moreover, the Lord will scatter you among all peoples, from one end of the earth to the other end of the earth" (Deuteronomy

28:64). "My God will cast them away because they have not listened to Him; and they will be wanderers among the nations" (Hosea 9:17).

God predicted that in the last days the nation Israel would be regathered to their homeland. Ezekiel 37:21 prophesies, "Behold, I will take the sons of Israel from among the nations where they have gone, and I will gather them from every side and bring them into their own land."

Prophecies regarding the nation of Israel's regathering are resplendent throughout the Bible. Listen to Ezekiel 38:8: "After many days you [Israel] will be summoned; in the latter years you will come into the land that is restored from the sword, whose inhabitants have been gathered from many nations to the mountains of Israel which had been a continual waste; but its people were brought out from the nations, and they are living securely, all of them."

Isaiah resounds with this prophetic truth of Israel's ultimate regathering as a nation. "Do not fear, for I am with you; I will bring your offspring from the east, and gather you from the west. I will say to the north, 'Give them up!' and to the south, 'Do not hold them back.' Bring My sons from afar, and My daughters from the ends of the earth" (Isaiah 43:5,6). Incredibly, after being bounced from one nation to the other for 2000 years the wandering Jews have regathered as a nation in their homeland! Even as you read this book, the Jews are still returning to Israel from every part of the globe. God's Word has been fulfilled precisely. Name one other nation to whom this has occurred after 2000 years. The odds are monumentally improbable for such a thing to happen.

What an awesome reminder to us that God's Word is true, and that every other prophetic claim of God will come to pass! Jesus Christ is going to return to the earth.

PROOF 6:
THE TRANSFORMED LIVES
OF CHRIST'S FOLLOWERS

Scripture says it simply, but beautifully: "If any man is in Christ, he is a new creature; the old things passed away; behold, new things have come" (2 Corinthians 5:17). The visible proof of Christ's return are the hundreds of millions of people who have been spiritually revolutionized by Jesus Christ.

He has delivered thousands of alcoholics, drug addicts, thieves, murderers, extortionists, liars, and psychopaths. These present-day trophies of grace remind us that God's Word is true, and that Jesus is coming again.

God has privileged me to meet so many of God's heroes. Of all the Christian celebrities, athletic stars, and entrepreneurs I have met, the one who made the most impact on my personal life was the great basketball star from LSU, Pistol "Pete" Maravich. Raised in Louisiana, Pistol Pete had an insatiable drive to be the best basketball player he could be. It was Pete's dad who taught him the disciplines which later made him unequaled as the foremost scorer in college basketball history.

Under his dad's coaching, Pete would dribble the ball when it was raining torrentially. He felt if he could control the ball in a strong downpour he could control it on the basketball court. Pete's dad would drive slowly down the road while Pete, in the passenger seat, would dribble the basketball with his long arm out the window. Who could ever forget those droopy socks on the playing field, a hallmark of the Pistol!

But after all the rewards, trophies, and ego adulation, Pete Maravich was empty. So disillusioned with life was he that he painted an emblem on his roof for a UFO to see. But his frustration turned to tranquility one memorable night when he recalls that God said to him, "Arise, take up thy strength." Finally the knowledge of Christ as his Savior made perfect sense. There in the middle of the night Pistol Pete was transformed by Jesus.

Pete took off spiritually like a locomotive. Everywhere he went he pointed people to Christ. When reporters asked basketball questions, he would shift to how much Jesus Christ meant to him.

I remember flying on a plane with Pete, watching him share Christ with the passenger next to him. He was so real, and such an inspiration to me every time he gave his testimony in one of our crusades.

Pete appeared on Larry King's TV show on the CNN network. Shortly thereafter Larry underwent heart bypass surgery. Of all the letters and gifts that King received after his surgery, he said none affected him as much as the one he received Monday, January 4, 1988. "In a package was a leather Bible with King's name embossed in gold on the cover. Enclosed was the following letter, dated December 31:

Dear Larry,

I'm so glad to hear that everything went well with your surgery. I want you to know that God was watching over you every minute, and even though I know you question that, I also know that one day it will be revealed to you. My prayer is that you remain open and God will touch your life as He has mine. Once I was a disbeliever. When I could not fill my life with basketball, I would simply substitute sex, liquid drugs or material things to feed my internal shell-like appearance. I was never satisfied. I have finally realized after

40 years that Jesus Christ is in me. He will reveal His truth to you Larry because He lives.

Pete Maravich 'Pistol Pete'

The day after King received that Bible, the 40-year-old Maravich . . . died of a heart attack while playing in a pickup basketball game."[4]

Irrefutably, Jesus Christ is going to return!

4

Characteristic Days of His Return

◆ ═══════════════════════════════════ ◆

As He was sitting on the Mount of Olives, the disciples came to Him privately, saying, 'Tell us, when will these things be, and what will be the sign of Your coming and of the end of the age?' And Jesus answered and said to them, 'See to it that no one misleads you, for many will come in My name, saying, "I am the Christ," and will mislead many. And you will be hearing of wars and rumors of wars; see that you are not frightened, for those things must take place, but that is not yet the end. For nation will rise against nation, and kingdom against kingdom, and in various places there will be famines and earthquakes. But all these things are merely the beginning of birth pangs. Then they will deliver you to tribulation, and will kill you, and you will be hated by all nations on account of My name. And at that time many will fall away and deliver up one another and hate one another. And many false prophets will arise, and will mislead many. And because lawlessness is increased most people's love will grow cold'" (Matthew 24:3-12).

Jesus' signs pointing to His second coming to the earth are very clear. His followers were curious; "How will we know when you are returning?" they asked.

"Lawlessness will abound," Christ responded. This is a prevalent end-time sign. Men and women will throw off spiritual and moral restraint. Society will be characterized by deception, evil, and fraud. Sin will abound.

TELLING THE TRUTH

The 1991 Prentice Hall book, *The Day America Told the Truth*, has received widespread media attention. Two thousand Americans, divided into nine quadrants and fifty locations (representing the entire United States), individually answered 1800 questions simultaneously in a five-day period. This was the most in-depth survey of American's true opinions ever conducted.

Authors James Patterson and Peter Kim relate the findings of their voluminous questionnaire.

> Americans are making up their own rules, their own laws. In effect, we're all making up our own moral codes. Only 13 percent of us believe in all of the Ten Commandments. There is absolutely no moral consensus in this country as there was in the 1950s, when all our institutions commanded more respect.
>
> We're not even honest with those we say we love. More than two-thirds of us would not confess a one-night stand to our spouses. Most people say that they've hidden their true feelings from a lover. The majority of us would not let our spouses or lovers question us if we were hooked up to a lie detector.
>
> A startling percentage of American children actually lose their virginity before the age of thirteen. Homosexual fantasies are common in every section of the United States. One in five of us, both men and women, have homosexual fantasies.

Just about everyone lies—91 percent of us lie regularly. Gays and bisexuals lie more than heterosexuals.

Our sex lives are actually pretty good, but we want more. This sexual hunger leads us to places and practices where the Bible and many federal and state laws explicitly tell us not to go. We couldn't care less. Two in every three men, and half of the women, said they wished that they could spend more time making love—but not with their current lovers.

Ninety-two percent of sexually active people report having had ten or more lovers, with a lifetime average of seventeen. Four in ten among us have had more than one lover in the past year. Singles get around much more. Since they became sexually active (by the age of sixteen for the majority), single people have averaged a four-above-par twenty-one lovers, four in the last year.

Marriage in the 1990s just doesn't mean what it always used to mean. This is true across America in every single region. The majority of men and women now believe in their hearts that it's a good idea to live together before marriage. And this fact may gladden the hearts of some lawyers: A thumping 59 percent of all Americans believe that it's a smart idea to draw up a prenuptial agreement, just in case. Thirty-six percent of Metropolitans were virgins on their wedding days vs. the national average of 29 percent.

Almost one-third of all married Americans (31 percent) have had or are now having an affair. This isn't a number from Hollywood or New York City. It's the national average for adultery.

One in five kids now lose their virginity before the age of 13. Children are actually launching another sexual revolution—one that is much deeper and more profound than the sexual liberation movement of the 1960s or 1970s. Overwhelmingly, the reason teenagers give for starting sex so early is the powerful force of peer pressure—peer pressure without any effective counterforce from many parents or from schools.

Almost as many, one in seven, confess that they were victims of sexual abuse as children. Extrapolating from our numbers, some 2.2 million Americans are reasonably certain that they have AIDS. That's just the beginning. Another 7 million people see themselves as being at very high risk for AIDS. The majority of those people, both those who are certain and those who believe that they are at high risk, are heterosexuals.

Alcohol is America's most serious drug by far. It has been that way for years. Close to 30 million Americans report having had a drinking problem. Over 19 million Americans admit that they have had serious alcohol problems in the past. Another 11 million of us are having alcohol problems right now. Alcohol abusers make trouble for others too: One-third of all adults have personally suffered from someone else's drinking.

As we enter the 1990s, only one American in five ever consult a minister, a priest, or a rabbi on everyday issues. Half of us haven't been to a religious service for a minimum of three months. One in three haven't been to a religious service for more than a year.

Sin, as most of us see it today, is doing unto others what we don't want done unto ourselves. Fewer than two people in five believe that sin is "going against God's will" or "violating the Ten Commandments." For the rest of us, sin is defined by our own consciences. We define what is sinful and what isn't.[1]

THE GENERATION AWAY FROM GOD

Predicting the end times, Paul warned that immorality, dishonesty, greed, rebellion, selfishness, unholiness, and much more would be correct adjectives depicting a generation that was away from God and would soon receive the Antichrist.

> But realize this, that in the last days difficult times will come. For men will be lovers of self, lovers of money, boastful, arrogant, revilers, disobedient to parents, ungrateful, unholy, unloving, irreconcilable, malicious gossips, without self-control, brutal, haters of good, treacherous, reckless, conceited, lovers of pleasure rather than lovers of God; holding to a form of godliness, although they have denied its power; and avoid such men as these (2 Timothy 3:1-5).

Could there be any more accurate description of our age than Paul's poignant words? He follows the thought in verse 13: "But evil men and impostors will proceed from bad to worse, deceiving and being deceived."

We live in a society that is increasingly repulsed by anyone saying "This is wrong" or "God forbids this type of activity." We tell our young people that it is their decision. If they feel like something is okay for them, fine. Sadly, there are very few Jeremiahs, Ezekiels, Isaiahs, or Daniels in our time who will stand up and point our nation away from the moral malaise in which she is sinking.

While a sleepy church seldom even notices, our youth, led by their outspoken icons, are veering from God into deep spiritual darkness.

Who has captured American youth and the media more than the 33-year-old sensation, Madonna. *Forbes'* front-cover homage presented her as the most sophisticated businesswoman in the country. She has made reportedly 125 million dollars in the last five years. Her 1991 "Truth or Dare" movie expresses her conviction that homosexuality and bisexuality are absolutely fine. Madonna's explicit "Justify My Love" video single, displaying her kissing with a woman and giving herself a sensual rubdown, sold 500,000 copies. (The video was so bad that even MTV banned it, but the public eagerly ate it up.)

USA Today senior planning editor Joe Urschel comments on the seductive bombshell:

> The kind of feeling you get when all your politically correct child-rearing leads your daughter to idolize Madonna. Naturally, from a father's perspective, I don't want my daughter to suffer stereotyping and sexism of earlier generations. And for me, that seems to be what Madonna represents.
>
> But maybe I'm just not thinking small enough. It's as easy to bash Madonna from a parental perspective as it is to think you can undo sexual stereotyping—genetic and cultural—with some balls and trucks. It's also just as smug. I wasn't much older than my daughter when the Beatles first appeared on Ed Sullivan. I remember turning immediately to my dad when their performance ended, saying without hesitation: "When I grow up, that's what I wanna do!" I remember the perplexed—almost disgusted—look on his face. Now,

almost 30 years later, does he not look at the Paul McCartney financial profile in *Fortune* magazine and wonder if he shouldn't have been more supportive of my musical aspirations?

Could I really learn to love Madonna?[2]

Maybe everything in America is now a question of money. Perhaps Mr. Urschel didn't read Madonna's two-part interview in *The Advocate*, the national Gay and Lesbian newsmagazine.

Tell me your whole history of working with gay people. I'd say that after my father, the most powerful, important relationship of my life was with Christopher Flynn, who was my ballet teacher, who was gay. I didn't understand the concept of gay at the time. I was probably 12 or 13 years old. All I knew was that my ballet teacher was different from everybody else. He was so alive. He had a certain theatricality about him. He made you proud of yourself, just the way he came up to me and put my face in his hand and said, "You are beautiful." No one had woken up that part of me yet. I was too busy being repressed by my Catholic father.

By the time I was 15 or 16, he took me to my first gay club to go dancing. I'd never been to a club. I'd only been to high school dances, and no guys would ever ask me to dance, because they thought I was insane, so I'd just go out and dance by myself.

They thought you were insane? Yes. In school and in my neighborhood and everything, I felt like such an outsider, a misfit, a weirdo. And suddenly when I went to the gay club, I didn't feel that way anymore. I just felt at home. I had a whole new sense of myself....

When Christopher introduced me to this life, I suddenly thought, that's not the only way that I have to be. I felt that my behavior was accepted around him.

I started spending a lot of time with dancers, and almost every male dancer that I knew was gay. Then I went through another kind of feeling inadequate because I was constantly falling in love with gay men. Of course, I was so miserable that I wasn't a man.... It would be so helpful for the straight community to see men in powerful positions coming out and saying "I'm gay" so they don't have these preconceived notions that all gay men are smarmy idiots living on the streets or whatever it is people think of gay men.

Why is the music industry so homophobic? They're not going to be when I get finished with them.... *Are you as kinky personally as your image makes you seem?* Well, what do you mean by kinky? I mean, I am aroused by two men kissing. Is that kinky? I am aroused by the idea of a woman making love to me while either a man or another woman watches.... There's Mary Magdalene—she was considered a fallen woman because she slept with men, but Jesus said it was O.K. I think they probably got it on, Jesus and Mary Magdalene. Those are my saint heroes.[3]

THE COMING JUDGMENT

Madonna will someday face the King of all kings and give an account for her lifestyle and influence. To suggest that Jesus and Mary "got it on" is nothing short of blasphemy. It was Jesus who said, "Every careless word that men shall speak, they shall render account for it in the day of judgment" (Matthew 12:36). I believe the two most awesome verses that relate to every person must be Luke 12:2,3: "There is nothing covered up that will not be revealed, and hidden that will not be known. Accordingly, whatever you have said in the dark shall be heard in the light, and what you have whispered in the inner rooms shall be proclaimed on the housetops." Standing before God, accompanied by a myriad of angels in attendance, every man and woman will give an account for every word which fell from his or her lips, and the influence which emanated from each life.

Jesus predicted His return with specific signs: "Just as it happened in the days of Noah, so it shall be also in the days of the Son of Man: They were eating, they were drinking, they were marrying, they were being given in marriage, until the day that Noah entered the ark, and the flood came and destroyed them all. It was the same as happened in the days of Lot: They were eating, they were drinking, they were buying, they were selling, they were planting, they were building; but on the day that Lot went out from Sodom it rained fire and brimstone from heaven and destroyed them all. It will be just the same on the day that the Son of Man is revealed" (Luke 17:26-30).

Jesus' message is simple and profound. During the days of Noah the wickedness was great, but no one was expecting judgment to fall. So it is in our time: The coming of Christ sounds absurd to the mainstream of life's inhabitants. Our society is gradually but predictably deteriorating because of sin.

With all the permissiveness that exists, kids want to kill themselves now more than ever before in the history of our nation. A recent Gallup Poll reported in *USA Today* said that one-third of all U.S. teenagers say they have considered suicide, 15 percent have thought seriously about it, and 6 percent have actually tried it.

Morally, our country and world are seriously adrift. Slowly the principles and faith which founded our nation are being left. We are emerging in a dark alley of colossal judgment. This is a journey predescribed in the Bible: Man will not eventually get better but will continue to degrade in sin and disease. It is this decadence and debauchery that will usher in the return of Jesus Christ.

DEATH IN THE MAKING

Kimberly Bergalis' skeletal, Holocaust-looking body continues to deteriorate in Florida. Weighing 65 pounds, just half of her previous body weight, she waits to die. Bergalis will be the first American to die of AIDS infected by her dentist, Dr. David Acer, according to the Centers for Disease Control. Dr. Richard Duff, a family doctor in Minneapolis, also waits for his imminent AIDS-related death. After a divorce in 1985, by his own admission he "chased around" and someone infected him. Yet Dr. Duff saw hundreds of patients who did not know he had AIDS until his resignation in 1991.

According to the CDC, as of March 31, 1991, 6436 health-care workers reported having AIDS: 1358 nurses, 703 physicians, 171 dentists and hygienists, and 1101 health aides. These are *reported* medical workers. But how many are unreported? Many for financial and professional reasons will not disclose their infection. Jesus said there would be an abundance of pestilences or diseases marking the time of His return. Epidemics will become widespread as we enter the final era of mankind on this planet. We read about the fourth seal broken with death riding on an ashen horse: "He who sat on it had the name Death; and Hades was following with him. And authority was given to them over a fourth of the earth, to kill with sword and with famine and with pestilence and by the wild beasts of the earth" (Revelation 6:8).

EARTHQUAKES AT THE END

Jesus also said that there would be earthquakes. The Loma Prieta earthquake occurred at 5:04 P.M. on October 17, 1990, in the San Francisco area. Measuring 7.1 on the Richter scale, this powerful quake was felt from Los Angeles to Nevada. It ranked among the strongest earthquakes in the U.S. in the twentieth century: 63 deaths, 3757 injuries, 12,000 people left homeless, damage totaling 10 billion dollars. At 11:41 A.M. on December 7, 1988, an earthquake registering 6.9 leveled the Armenian town of Spitak, as well as half the buildings in Kirovakan. The death toll was almost 25,000 people. On September 19, 1985, Mexico City's devastating earthquake collapsed 250 buildings; 10,000 people died and 30,000 were injured.

The U.S. Geological Survey predicts that there is now a 60 percent chance of a magnitude 7.5 or larger earthquake—"The Big One"—on the San Adreas Fault near Southern California in the next 30 years. Shockingly, seismologists believe that the deadliest earthquakes could actually occur on smaller faults that run directly under city streets, oil refineries, dams, high-rise buildings, and other urban structures sited in California right now. What would a major quake in Los Angeles be like? According to the experts, most high-rise buildings would ride out the shaking, though swaying dramatically; however, 7900 unreinforced pre-1960 buildings would collapse; most of the notorious L.A. freeways would be hopeless cesspools of thousands of accidents; hundreds of thousands of homes would collapse or slide off their foundations (with flying furniture killing or injuring an inestimable number of people); fewer than one in ten telephone calls would go through; 1200 water mains would rupture, causing mass flooding; the Castaic Dam above L.A. would kill 15,000 people and potentially leave 143,000 homeless.

MENTAL ILLNESS AND SUBSTANCE ABUSE

But it is the young generation that I am the most concerned about. There are 24 million young people in the United States, representing 7 percent of our nation's population. It is this group of people which so clearly reveal the change in values and our failure to evangelize. A report by the Institute of Medicine estimates that as many as 7.5 million children suffer from some form of psychological illness:

> A federal survey shows that after remaining constant for ten years, hospitalizations of youngsters with psychiatric disorders jumped from 81,500 to about 112,000 between 1980 and 1986. What is causing so much mental anguish? The sad truth is that a growing number of American youngsters have home lives that are hostile to healthy emotional growth. According to a report in June by a commission formed by the American Medical Association and the National Association of State Boards of Education, about 10 percent of teenage boys and 18 percent of girls try to kill themselves at least once.[4]

Record numbers of kids are in treatment. It is impossible to answer these acute youth problems without the spiritual dimension. Diane S. Lund in *The Psychiatric Times, Medicine and Behavior* reports that American Psychiatric Association surveys reveal that about half of all U.S. psychiatrists are either agnostics or atheists. (Sigmund Freud called any belief in God delusional, stating that religious beliefs represented a neurotic wish for a father. Freud still influences psychiatrists today.)

Drug abuse in our society and internationally seems to be a plague which has no cure. Close to our nation's capital is a drug war zone almost leading all the other states. Industrial leaders claim that drug and alcohol abuse have led to economic losses totaling over 100 billion dollars a year, not to mention the thousands of needless deaths and the thousands of children born hooked. The National Association for Perinatal Addiction Research and Education estimates that as many as 375,000 children will be harmed by their mother's drug use during pregnancy. The study reports that 11 percent of all women giving birth use one or more illegal drugs during pregnancy.

These societal maladies indicate that God's Word is true: Jesus Christ is going to return. Our preoccupation with sensuality, self-centeredness, and evil is a graphic fulfillment of biblical prophecy. Once-Christian America has defied God in spite of the spiritual light He has shed on this republic, and in a sense we are tempting God to judge us. This deplorable condition is the accenting mark that Christ's coming is very soon.

5

Apocalyptic Apostasy

◆ ══════════════ ◆

The Spirit explicitly says that in later times some will fall away from the faith, paying attention to deceitful spirits and doctrines of demons, by means of the hypocrisy of liars seared in their own conscience as with a branding iron" (1 Timothy 4:1,2).

"Now we request you, brethren, with regard to the coming of our Lord Jesus Christ and our gathering together to Him, that you may not be quickly shaken from your composure or be disturbed either by a spirit or a message or a letter as if from us, to the effect that the day of the Lord has come. Let no one in any way deceive you, for it will not come unless the apostasy comes first, and the man of lawlessness is revealed, the son of destruction" (2 Thessalonians 2:1-3).

"Let us not sleep as others do, but let us be alert and sober" (1 Thessalonians 5:6).

"I know your deeds, that you are neither cold or hot; I would that you were cold or hot. So because you are lukewarm, and neither hot nor cold, I will spit you out of My mouth.... You say, 'I am rich, and have become wealthy, and have need of nothing,' and you do not know that you are wretched and miserable and poor and blind and naked. ... Behold, I stand at the door and knock; if anyone hears My voice and opens the door, I will come in to him, and will dine with him, and he with Me" (Revelation 3:15-17,20).

"For certain persons have crept in unnoticed, those who were long beforehand marked out for this condemnation, ungodly persons who turn the grace of God into licentiousness and deny our only Master and Lord, Jesus Christ" (Jude 4).

GROWING APOSTASY

One predominant sign pointing to the return of Jesus Christ is the growing apostasy within the Christian community. The term "apostasy" simply means a falling away from the true faith.

This falling away from the faith is quite different from willfully rejecting Jesus Christ or God's inspired Word. Those people are unbelievers, or as Jude says, "clouds without water" (Jude 12). They don't know God.

An apostate is someone who knows all about God and Jesus Christ, but falls away from obedient faith. This is very different from false belief resulting from ignorance.

One of the griefs of my heart has been to witness the host of people I have personally known who have fallen. So many of them have been ministers, men who knew better. Yet Satan got the upper hand. When I first began to speak and travel in evangelism I was a young Youth for Christ evangelist. The thrill of my heart was preaching the gospel anywhere God would let me. I was somewhat naive.

I must confess that I have been absolutely jarred at the number of preachers who have committed spiritual treason. Because I am an evangelist, and have spoken in over

1100 churches throughout North America, most of my perspective has been directed toward ministers. If ministers are indulging in sin as I have observed, what is happening in the lives of laity, who are not required to deliver spiritually on a weekly basis?

Tales of homosexuality, financial scandals, and extensive extramarital sexual activity are commonplace. If people really knew what was going on behind the scenes with some nationally known ministers of the gospel, they would be floored.

In a sense, some of the proponents of evangelical Christianity have been the greatest hindrances in convincing an unbelieving world of the redemptive message. Charles Shepard's 635-page book *Forgiven* (Atlantic Monthly Press) should be read by every person wanting to be an evangelist for Jesus Christ. Appropriately, Shepard quotes a private letter from Pat Robertson to Jim Bakker dated September 15, 1977: "Jim, God does not bless falsehood, and the Bible says He resists the proud.... Unless you face reality and ask God's forgiveness, He is going to bring you down. God is speaking to you through things that are happening. I pray that you will get His message."

How shallow and cheap our presentation of the gospel has become by the inconsistency and unholiness of our lives! God forgive us and draw us to our knees! Peter boldly pointed the blame: "For it is time for judgment to begin with the household of God; and if it begins with us first, what will be the outcome for those who do not obey the gospel of God?" (1 Peter 4:17).

REVIVAL ON THE BRINK

The godly, irreplaceable Leonard Ravenhill has written much on the critical need of a Spirit-empowered revival.

Never will I forget the day I sat with him in his home in Lindale, Texas, and drank in every word he said. Finally I knew my time was up when his five intercessors came to pray with him. This was nothing new; Ravenhill has spent days on end with these holy people storming God's throne for an unprecedented move of the Spirit.

To take an overall view of the Church today leaves one wondering how much longer a holy God can refrain from implementing His threat to spew this Laodicean thing out of His mouth. For if there is one thing preachers are agreed upon, it is that this is the Laodicean age in the Church.

Yet while over our heads hangs the Damoclean sword of rejection, we believers are lean, lazy, luxury-loving, loveless, and lacking. Though our merciful God will pardon our sins, purge our iniquity, and pity our ignorance, our lukewarm hearts are an abomination in His sight. We must be hot or cold, flaming or freezing, burning out or cast out. Lack of heat and lack of love God hates.

Christ is now "wounded in the house of His friends." The holy Book of the living God suffers more from its exponents today than from its opponents!

We are loose in the use of scriptural phrases, lopsided in interpreting them, and lazy to the point of impotence in appropriating their measureless wealth. Mr. Preacher will wax eloquent in speech and fervent in spirit, serving the Lord with vigor and perspiration to defend the Bible's inspiration. Yet that same dear man a few breaths later with deadly calmness will be heard rationalizing that same inspired Word by outdating its miracles and by firmly declaring: "This text is not for today." Thus the new believer's warm faith is doused with the ice water of the preacher's unbelief.

The Church alone can "limit the Holy One of Israel," and today she has consummate skill in doing it. If there are degrees in death, then the deadest I know of is to preach about the Holy Ghost without the anointing of the Holy Ghost.[1]

THE DYING FERVOR

Slowly our message has changed, and along with it the fervor of our faith. *U.S. News & World Report* ran a front-cover feature story on "The Rekindling of Hell." Surprisingly, 60 percent of people polled in 1990 stated their belief in a hell. In 1952 it was 58 percent. Far more believed in heaven, of course. Seventy-eight percent in 1990 stated their belief in heaven, compared to 72 percent in 1952. Three out of five Americans now believe in hell.

Tragically, very few ministers are bold enough to present this reality to those they minister to.

In many churches, one finds little talk these days about a literal, punitive hell as a real possibility after death. "My congregation would be stunned to hear a sermon on hell," says the Rev. Mary Kraus, pastor of the Dumbarton United Methodist Church in Washington, D.C. Her parishioners, she says, are "upper-middle-class, well-educated critical thinkers" who view God as "compassionate and loving, not someone who's going to push them into eternal damnation."

Now, to many scholars, a literal hell is "part of an understanding of the cosmos that just doesn't exist anymore," says Stephen J. Patterson, professor of New

Testament at Eden Theological Seminary in St. Louis. Biblical references to hell are often viewed metaphorically as referring to the isolation, pain and suffering that result from evil. "Once we discovered we could create hell on earth," says John Dominic Crossan of DePaul University in Chicago, "it became silly to talk about it in a literal sense."

In Roman Catholicism, the possibility of hell for the wicked remains on the doctrinal books. But according to modern teachings, few souls are likely to end up there. Since the 1960's, when a spirit of ecumenism took hold of the Church at the Second Vatican Council, Catholic theology has emphasized the potential for all souls ultimately to make it to heaven—although many first may have to spend time in purgatory, a temporary lodging where sinners are rehabilitated. In earlier times, "we were told hell was a real possibility for all of us," recalls the Rev. Richard McBrien, chairman of theology at the University of Notre Dame. "If you ate a hot dog on Friday and got hit by a truck before you went to confession, you'd suffer the same punishment as if you were a murderer." Now, says the Rev. Avery Dulles, theology professor at Fordham University in New York, the emphasis is on the mercy and love of God.[2]

Some evangelicals today have become too cowardly to reveal God's truth regarding eternity, and man's fate in rejecting Jesus Christ as Lord and Savior. How different we are from a Luther, who stood against the whole world for spiritual change! How different from a Daniel, who would not compromise in the most wicked city in the world at the time!

American church historian Martin Marty observes:

Meantime, hell disappeared. And no one noticed. For liberal Protestants, hell began to fade in the 19th century along with Calvinism's stern and predestining God. In once-Puritan New England, the Universalists decided that God is much too good to condemn anyone to hell, while the Unitarians concluded that humanity is much too good for God to punish—if, indeed, there is a God. Today, hell is theology's H-word, a subject too trite for serious scholarship. When he prepared a Harvard lecture on the disappearance of hell, Marty consulted the indices of several scholarly journals, including one dating back to 1889, and failed to find a single entry.

Even conservative evangelicals are losing their taste for fire and brimstone. At the core of evangelicalism is the belief that one must accept Jesus Christ as personal Lord and Savior or suffer in hell for all eternity. There is no purgatory for minor sinners or limbo for those good souls who never had the Gospel preached to them in this life. But now, says University of Virginia sociologist James Hunter, author of two books on contemporary evangelicalism, "many evangelicals have a difficult time conceiving of people, especially virtuous nonbelievers, going to hell." Hunter asked evangelical students if they thought Gandhi was in hell. "They recognized that by their own theology Gandhi should be in hell, but the idea made them extremely nervous," Hunter says. "They recognized that to say a good man like Gandhi is in hell is to say that friends of theirs who are not born again will also go to hell, and socially that's a difficult position to maintain." As a result of this social conflict, he concludes that evangelicals are tempering their images of hell: "People say now, 'I think there is a hell but I hope it will be a soul-sleep.'"

At Harvard Divinity School, theologian Gordon Kaufman traces four centuries of decline in the concepts of heaven and hell; what is left is intellectually empty baggage. "It seems to me we've gone through irreversible changes," Kaufman declares, "I don't think there can be any future for heaven and hell."[3]

HOLDING DOCTRINAL INTEGRITY

I certainly don't advocate a rude, simplistic, "turn-or-burn" approach to evangelism. When I spoke at the National Religious Broadcasters Convention in Washington D.C. in January of 1991, I was outspoken that we needed to culturally identify with the audience we are attempting to reach with the gospel. This is biblical; Paul commended this technique in 1 Corinthians 9:19-23.

However, we must not lose doctrinal integrity in our zeal to persuade men to Christ. Jesus is our example in all manners of faith and practice. Christ preached on hell more than any other New Testament writer. Given *koine* Greek's preciseness, one has to be reckless to twist Jesus' definition of the afterlife.

Again, we must be aggressive, innovative, and relevant. We hear much today about the megachurch. It has been my privilege to preach in scores of them all over the continent.

Megachurches are remaking the country's religious landscape. Indeed, says the Rev. Lyle Schaller, a United Methodist minister and renowned church consultant, the megachurch represents one of the "most significant changes taking place in American Protestantism in the second half of the 20th century."

While most Protestant denominations are in slow but steady decline, megachurches are springing up from

Montgomery, Alabama, to Chicago. And some say they are hastening the demise of traditional churches.[4]

These churches are growing because they preach the truth of God's Word in a loving, empowered, honest manner. I have noticed that, regardless of the denominational affiliation, the pastors all have the exact same common denominators: They are men of integrity, passion for the lost, innovativity, and communication skills, and they are biblical literalists unashamed to stand for God.

LOSING INTEGRITY

Some churches are attempting to reach people by cultural identification to the extent of losing their biblical integrity.

Newsweek's front-cover feature on December 17, 1990, blared, AND THE CHILDREN SHALL LEAD THEM: Young Americans Return to God. But to what kind of church are they returning? Is it one in allegiance with the biblical mandate, or one which Satan has cleverly counterfeited?

This is the 1990's, an age of mix'em, match'em salad-bar spirituality—Quaker-palians, charismatic Catholics, New Age Jews—where brand loyalty is a doctrine of the past and the customer is king.

What counts on the Sabbath Day, if a church or synagogue is to attract its share of the baby-boom market, is not the name on the door but the programs inside. All Saints (Episcopal Church, Pasadena, CA), for example, bills itself at least 20 "ministries of compassion," from the AIDS Service Center and the Union Station Homeless Shelter to GALAS, a gay and lesbian fellowship.

Above all, however, the return to religion is fueled by the boomers' experiences of becoming parents—and the realization that children need a place where they can learn solid values and make friends with peers who share them.

At one time or another, roughly two-thirds of baby boomers dropped out of organized religion. But in recent years, more than one-third of the dropouts have returned. About 57 percent—43 million people—now attend church or synagogue. More than 80 percent of the boomers consider themselves religious and believe in life after death. The biggest group of returnees (about 60 percent) are married with children. The least likely to have returned are married couples without kids.

According to the best study to date funded by the Lily Endowment, one-third never left church at all; many merely switched denominational allegiance. The most steadfast of these "loyalists," reports sociologists Wade Clark Roof of the University of California, Santa Barbara, are conservative Protestants—people who were less mobile in their youth, less likely to attend college and, even when they did, less prone to taking up alternative lifestyles and enthusiasms. By contrast, liberal mainline Protestants suffered a serious hemorrhage—as many as one in four Methodists and Presbyterians switched allegiance or dropped religion entirely. Roman Catholics in and out, are becoming highly selective in what they will accept. And Jews have yet to recover 70 percent of their lost generation. Altogether, Roof concludes, about 43 percent are still unchurched—though most say they believe in some kind of God—and 24 percent are returnees to the institutional fold.

For keepers of the citadels of faith, it is these return-ing sheep—all 18 million—who offer the greatest challenge. Their eldest, now in their 40s, are easiest to understand.

For earlier generations, the service was a stitch in time to hear the familiar word of God and to get right with the Lord. Those Sundays are gone.... Unlike earlier religious revivals, the aim this time (aside from born-again traditionalists of all faiths) is support not salvation, help rather than holiness, a circle of spiri-tual equals rather than an authoritative church or guide. A group affirmation of self is at the top of the agenda, which is why some of the least demanding churches are now in greatest demand.[5]

DENYING THE POWER

Relating to the impending second coming of Jesus Christ, Paul had a description of religious people in the end times: "Holding to a form of godliness, although they have denied its power; and avoid such men as these" (2 Timothy 3:5).

Paul repeatedly reminded the Christians in Thessalonica of Christ's return. He exhorted them to be obedient and busy serving the Master. He warned, "If anyone does not obey our instruction in this letter, take special note of that man and do not associate with him, so that he may be put to shame" (2 Thessalonians 3:14).

George Gallup in his book *Religion in the 90's* points out that young people (15-24 years of age) are less interested in religion than their parents by a ratio of two to one. I am afraid the young generation today has not seen a genuine moving of God's Spirit. They go to rock concerts empow-ered by lights, sound, music, and movement. The icons of the young too often tell kids to do or experience what they feel is right for them. Sadly, the few that do attend church enter an atmosphere that is boring and often totally irrelevant to their hurts and problems. If only they could enter a church supercharged with the power of God!

America's largest Protestant denomination, the Southern Baptist Convention, reports an almost 50 percent decline in youth baptisms in the last 15 years! (In 1972 Southern Baptists baptized 137,667 young people compared to 80,704 in 1989.)[6] Church leaders are worried: What is going wrong? Leaders have launched YOUTH-REACH in an attempt to turn the tide.

When prayer is absent the church moves in backward motion.

> Throughout the 1970s and 1980s the churches [in Britain] lost so many members that researchers came to study church growth in reverse. Figures by Marc Europe reveal that this rush for the church doors peaked between 1979 and 1985. The average loss of adult members was 45,000 per year in this period. Between 1985 and 1989 the drain was down to 12,000 per year. All of which adds up to a serious loss from a grand total in 1979 of only 4 million members including Protestants and Catholics—in a population of 56 million.[7]

WHEN GOD'S PEOPLE PRAY

Church growth and evangelism spread like a prairie fire when God's people pray. Of the largest megachurches in the world right now, eight are located in Seoul, South Korea. The church in Korea emphasizes prayer far more than our U.S. congregations. No wonder God is moving as He is! The largest church in the world, Yoido Full Gospel Church in Seoul, is growing at a rate of 10,000 members a month! And it averages a weekly attendance of 180,000, according to church-growth analyst Dr. John Vaughan. Six other congregations have an average weekly attendance of 50,000 or more. One South Korean minister comments on the church's dependency on prayer.

> Not only in our church, but in most churches in Korea, our prayer time begins at 5:00 A.M. We regularly pray for one or two hours. After our prayer time, we begin the normal routines of our day. Since the most important thing in our lives is prayer, we have learned to retire early. On Fridays, we spend the entire night in prayer. Many of our visitors are surprised to see our church packed with people for our all-night prayer meeting.
>
> On Sundays, before each one of our seven services, we spend time in prayer. I am shocked when I visit churches that have social gatherings before Sunday services.... During our Sunday services, the believers pray together. The sound of thousands of Korean believers praying together reminds me of the thunderous roar of a mighty waterfall.
>
> I usually wake up between 4:30 and 5:00 in the morning. Of course, when I conducted our early morning prayer meetings at the church, I used to get up earlier. However, many of my associate pastors anxiously await their turn to lead our early morning prayer time, so I normally can stay at home very early in the morning.[8]

With all the ministers in America alone, think of what would happen here if a prayer revival began!

6

Pivotal Israel: Beckoning the Second Coming

◆ ═══════════════════════ ◆

*I will make you a great nation, and I will bless you,
and make your name great; and so you shall be a
blessing; and I will bless those who bless you, and the
one who curses you I will curse. And in you all the
families of the earth shall be blessed.*

—Genesis 12:2,3

No area of Bible prophecy substantiates the return of the Lord Jesus Christ more dramatically and is more mentally stimulating than the topic of the nation of Israel. It can send a tingle down your spine to comprehend the exactness of God's Word regarding this impossible-to-extinguish nation of Jewish people.

Don't let me lose you in this chapter; put on your thinking cap and follow with me for a thrilling recognition of God's preservation and future plans for His covenant people.

ISRAEL IN THE PAST

It was over 4000 years ago, according to the Scriptures, that God promised a believing and obedient Abraham (the very first Jew) a land flowing with milk and honey. History proves that for centuries Abraham and his descendants lived in the land now called Israel.

God set up a divine covenant with Abraham. The word "covenant" means a pledge or promise. For centuries God has been obligated by this covenant, which was both personal (toward Abraham) and national (toward Israel). God promised a special spiritual relationship and a geographic land space for His chosen nation.

> I will make you a great nation, and I will bless you, and make your name great, and so you shall be a blessing; and I will bless those who bless you, and the one who curses you I will curse. And in you all the families of the earth shall be blessed (Genesis 12:2,3).

This covenant has been termed "the Abrahamic covenant." It is an everlasting, abiding, irrevocable covenant from the Lord to the nation of Israel. (See also Genesis 13:14-18; 15:18; 17:1-8; 22:16-18).

God has a special love for Israel:

> You are a holy people to the Lord your God; the Lord your God has chosen you to be a people for His own possession out of all the peoples who are on the face of the earth. The Lord did not set His love on you nor choose you because you were more in number than any of the peoples, for you were the fewest of all peoples, but because the Lord loved you and kept the oath which He swore to your forefathers, the Lord brought you out by a mighty hand, and redeemed you from the house of slavery, from the hand of Pharaoh king of Egypt (Deuteronomy 7:6-8; see also Deuteronomy 14:2; 1 Chronicles 17:22).

During a deathly drought, the Jews left for Egypt and later became enslaved by pagan Egyptian pharaohs for centuries. Sovereignly, God raised up Moses to deliver His people, and their exodus is one of the most exciting parts of the Bible to read (see the book of Exodus).

Prior to entering the Promised Land, Moses reminded the Israelites of God's covenant relationship with them: "That you may enter into the covenant with the Lord your God, and into His oath which the Lord your God is making with you today, in order that He may establish you today as His people and that He may be your God, just as He spoke to you and as He swore to your fathers, to Abraham, Isaac, and Jacob" (Deuteronomy 29:12,13). As humans we often default on our promises, but God has never defaulted on the nation of Israel.

Much of man's present-day moral code is based upon the Ten Commandments, originally given to Moses on Mount Sinai. Finally, after a 40-year disobedience delay by the Israelites, Joshua led them across the Jordan River into the Promised Land.

For almost 2000 years Israel was the heart of Jewish life. Contemporary archeological evidences remind us of a Jewish nation which was the envy and fear of surrounding nations.

In approximately 952 B.C. King Solomon, David's son, built a breathtaking temple in Jerusalem. Activated by the Jewish people's disobedience to God's revealed plan, in 585 B.C. the Babylonians destroyed the temple. Again, this captivity and temple destruction was prophesied in advance by Jeremiah: "This whole land shall be a desolation and a horror, and these nations shall serve the king of Babylon seventy years" (Jeremiah 25:11). Fifty years later God softened the pagan king's heart and the Jews were allowed to rebuild their temple.

Following centuries of prosperity, the Roman army conquered Jerusalem and destroyed the temple, with the exception of its foundation stones (still visible today). This cataclysmic destruction was prophesied by Jesus Christ: "When He [Jesus] approached, He saw the city and wept over it saying, 'If you had known in this day, even you, the things which make for peace! But now they have been hidden from your eyes. For the days shall come upon you when your enemies will throw up a bank before you, and surround you, and hem you in on every side, and will level you to the ground and your children within you, and they will not leave in you one stone upon another, because you did not recognize the time of your visitation'" (Luke 19:41-44). The Jews were subsequently sent into exile, and the Romans changed the land's name from Israel to Palestine (reportedly because of the Philistines living in the south).

God had warned Israel of a worldwide dispersion if they were disobedient to His commands: "It shall come about that as the Lord delighted over you to prosper you and multiply you, so the Lord will delight over you to make you perish and destroy you; and you shall be torn from the land where you are entering to possess it. Moreover, the Lord will scatter you among all peoples, from one end of the earth to the other end of the earth" (Deuteronomy 28:63, 64).

History notes that for 2000 years Palestine was ruled by numerous foreign conquerors. These included the Byzantines, Muslim Arabs, European Crusaders, and Ottomans. Very few Jews lived there; as a whole they were scattered throughout different parts of the world.

ISRAEL IN THE PRESENT

Yuri Grandel, 16, a recent immigrant to Israel from the

Soviet Union, was quoted as saying, "Israel is the only place I feel at home. It is my country because it is a Jewish country. I finally feel like I belong somewhere." Unceasingly, Jerusalem and the land of Israel has remained the focus of Jews for their culture and religion.

The chances of an entire nation of people regathering after 2000 years of exile and persecution presents odds that run off the scale. Nevertheless, in exact fulfillment of Bible prophecy, the nation of Israel was formally reestablished on May 14, 1948, as Zionist leader David Ben-Gurion proclaimed the new State of Israel. Here again we see God's prophetic Word fulfilled. Listen to Hosea 3:4,5: "For the sons of Israel will remain for many days without king or prince, without sacrifice or sacred pillar, and without ephod or household idols. Afterward the sons of Israel will return and seek the Lord their God and David their king; and they will come trembling to the Lord and to His goodness in the last days." (See also Deuteronomy 30:1-3; Isaiah 11:11,12; Ezekiel 36:23,24).

Nowhere can we see the hand of God more clearly than in Israel. Consider the formidable steps which led to this reestablishment.

Zionism was a political movement which sprang up in Europe in the late 1800's. Its goal was to recreate a homeland for the Jewish people in Palestine. But this seemed an impossibility. The Embassy of Israel reports the following notable steps:

- ✦ By 1914, 60,000 Jews had emigrated to Palestine, increasing the residential total to 85,000.

- ✦ Towns and villages were established, with trees planted, etc.

- ✦ Concurrently, 30,000 Arabs enticed by the country's rapid economic growth and job opportunities settled there. Total Arab population: 500,000.

- ✦ The League of Nations, following World War I, awarded jurisdiction over Palestine to Great Britain. This organized ¾ of Palestine into what is today the State of Jordan.

- ✦ Great Britain's promise was clear: "to facilitate the establishment in Palestine of a national home for Jewish people." Tenacious Arab pressure caused Britain to abandon its pledge.

- ✦ Infamy's years, 1939-1945, saw madman Adolf Hitler, backed by Nazi Germany, mercilessly exterminate 6,000,000 Jews. Again survivors of the Holocaust looked to Palestine as their refuge.

- ✦ In 1947, world opinion and Britain's release of Palestine favored establishment of a Jewish homeland.

- ✦ The United Nations, by a 33-to-13 vote, partitioned Palestine west of the Jordan River into two parts, one for the Jews and one for the Arabs. The Jews were unanimous, the Arabs dissenting.

- ✦ Israel's Declaration of Independence says, "We offer peace and unity to all the neighboring states and their peoples, and invite them to cooperate with the independent Jewish nation for the common good of all."

Tragically, since 1949 Israel has been kept in a state of war by its neighbors and has been engaged four times in full-scale combat. Once Iraq attempted to get Israel involved in war.

+ October, 1956: Egypt nationalized the Suez Canal and blockaded the Strait of Tiran, cutting off access to the Israeli port of Eilat.

+ June, 1967: Israel defended itself against attacks by the newly formed PLO, Jordan, Syria, and threatening Egypt.

+ 1973: During Yom Kippur, Egypt and Syria attacked Israel. Against the odds, Israel prevailed.

+ 1982: Israel moved against PLO attacks.

+ 1991: Iraq's Scud missiles hit Israel repeatedly by Saddam Hussein's order as he attempted to lure Israel into the war with the United States. Israel refrained.

In 1979, Israel and Egypt made peace as President Jimmy Carter mediated a formal signed treaty. Yet other Arab nations surrounding Israel refuse their right of existence.

Uniquely, Israel has been preserved against all odds. Why? Because God Himself is on Israel's side; eternally they are His chosen people: "'I will also plant them on their land, and they will not again be rooted out from their land which I have given them, says the Lord your God'" (Amos 9:15). According to the Bible, no nation or army will uproot Israel from their regathered homeland. Any nation which attempts to fight against Israel now will find themselves fighting against God!

+ Following May 14, 1948, Israel was attacked by Iraq, Lebanon, Syria, Jordan, and Egypt. Incredibly, after gruesome battles Israel victoriously won its War of Independence. (Jordanian soldiers remained in occupation of what they called the West Bank, biblical Judea and Samaria. Egyptian troops held the Gaza Strip.)

So we see that Israel has survived the opposition and brutality of centuries. Today Israel numbers 4.8 million people, 90 percent of whom live in cities and towns. Jerusalem is Israel's capital city, just as it was 3000 years ago under the reign of King David. Tel Aviv, Israel's second-largest city, is a bustling metropolis considered to be the entertainment capital of the country.

Israel's 4.8 million inhabitants are divided into 83 percent Jewish and 17 percent Muslim or Christian. This excludes, of course, the Muslim group of Judea and Samaria. In 1990 alone, 181,000 immigrants from the Soviet Union were assimilated into Israel. Jewish people are migrating from all over the world to Israel. This small country has about the same land mass as the state of Maryland. An eight-hour drive through Israel will take you from the snow-covered mountains in the north to the desert in the south. In the middle one can enjoy a refreshing swim on the sunny beaches of the Mediterranean.

There are many remarkable prophecies that relate to the nation of Israel. Some have not been fulfilled as yet, but with Israel following the divine timetable, we know that it is but a matter of time.

THE TIMES OF THE GENTILES

"They will fall by the edge of the sword, and will be led captive into all the nations; and Jerusalem will be trampled under foot by the Gentiles until the times of the Gentiles be fulfilled" (Luke 21:24).

In the Greek language the word "fulfilled" is the same as "finished." This prophecy clearly and simply means that the times of Gentile world-rule will be consummated when Jerusalem is no longer under Gentile control.

But Jerusalem is already in Jewish hands, and the Jews have returned to Israel. What is the discrepancy? Listen to 2 Chronicles 6:6: "I have chosen Jerusalem that My name might be there, and I have chosen David to be over My people Israel."

What is Jerusalem to God? Jerusalem is not roads, homes, and buildings. Jerusalem is a *temple*, where God's glory dwells, where His people come to Him through sacrifice, where He meets them. "Then it shall come about that the place in which the Lord your God shall choose for His name to dwell, there you shall bring all that I command you: your burnt offerings and your sacrifices, your tithes and the contribution of your hand, and all your choice votive offerings which you will vow to the Lord" (Deuteronomy 12:11).

This was not just any place in Jerusalem; it was a divinely chosen spot. According to 2 Chronicles 3:1 it was on Mount Moriah. This was the exact spot that God told David to purchase from Ornan the Jebusite, and to erect an altar on it (see 1 Chronicles 21:18). One thousand years earlier Abraham prepared to offer his son, Isaac, as a sacrifice on this same sacred spot (see Genesis 22:2). Interestingly, this place is very close to Calvary, where Jesus Christ was crucified.

The *new* city of Jerusalem did go back to the Jews, but the *old* city, including the all-important temple site on Mount Moriah, has remained in the hands of Jordanian Arabs. This is the one spot in Jerusalem still in control by Gentile hands. The Arabs have built their Dome of the Rock on

Mount Moriah itself! It stands like a volcanic trigger between Jews and Arabs. To the Muslim world it is the second-most-holy place in existence.

And so we see that the prophecy of Luke 21:24 has yet to be fulfilled. When will it be fulfilled? When Jesus Christ returns to planet Earth and sets up His eternal kingdom: "I saw heaven opened; and behold, a white horse, and He who sat upon it is called Faithful and True; and in righteousness He judges and wages war" (Revelation 19:11).

ISRAEL IN THE TRIBULATION

God is not finished with the nation of Israel; His covenant is everlasting. Sadly, we see the nation of Israel clearly depicted in the tribulation, that seven-year period after the rapture of the church (Christians) from the earth. There are many significant tribulation passages, but let me point your attention to two key passages.

"He [the Antichrist] will make a firm covenant with the many for one week [this term means seven years], but in the middle of the week [3 1/2 years] he will put a stop to sacrifice and grain offering; and on the wing of abominations will come one who makes desolate, even until a complete destruction, one that is decreed, is poured out on the one who makes desolate" (Daniel 9:27).

The seven-year tribulation really centers around the nation of Israel. It has been called "Jacob's time of trouble." Jeremiah 30:7 says, "Alas! for that day is great, there is none like it; and it is the time of Jacob's distress."

The tribulation is going to be a time of severe judgement, and Israel is going to be in the very center of it.

> ✦ According to Revelation chapter 7 and onward, Israel is clearly seen *in* the tribulation. A group

from every tribe of Israel will begin to propagate the repentance message (Revelation 7:4). God will raise up 144,000 Jewish evangelists who had been converted from unbelief. They will be "sealed," which means protected from the Antichrist's destructive system. They won't be able to be killed!

♦ According to Revelation 11:8, the Antichrist's world headquarters will be in Jerusalem! "Their dead bodies will lie in the street of the great city which mystically is called Sodom and Egypt, where also their Lord was crucified." Unquestionably, the Antichrist's maniacal system is headquartered in Jerusalem. Notice verse 13: "In that hour there was a great earthquake, and a tenth of the city fell; and seven thousand people were killed in the earthquake, and the rest were terrified and gave glory to the God of heaven." The Greek term here is "men of renown" or what we would call world leaders. When Jerusalem is rocked by an earthquake many notable leaders will be killed.

♦ According to Revelation 12:13, Israel is viewed by the figure of a woman. And the woman gave birth to the child, figurative of Christ. The dragon unmistakably represents Satan. Satan is going to persecute Israel during the tribulation (see Revelation 12:14).

♦ Matthew 24:15-51 is an extremely clear picture of the tribulation, and the nation of Israel is there! Verse 16 says, "Then let those who are in Judea flee to the mountains." Geographically, that is Israel! Jesus said, "Therefore when you see the abomination of desolation which was spoken of through Daniel the prophet, standing in the holy place, let the reader understand" (verse 15). This prophetic utterance by Christ corresponds directly with Daniel 9:27. The Antichrist is going to make a covenant with the Jews, with Israel. When? At the beginning of the seventieth week, the beginning of the tribulation. This world leader will reactivate temple worship through this covenant. The Jews will be ecstatic! However, in the middle of the week, ($3\frac{1}{2}$ years) everything will change. The Antichrist will destroy the temple worship. He himself will enter the rebuilt Jewish temple, proclaim himself as God, and demand that he be worshiped. That is exactly what Jesus meant by the term "the abomination of desolation." What will the response be? Matthew 24:16: *flee*. A number of the Jews will head for secrecy and protection. And this will last for $3\frac{1}{2}$ years.

The regathering of the nation of Israel which is presently taking place is preliminary to what will occur at the end of the tribulation. At the second coming of Christ all of Israel will be regathered. This is emphatically predicted in Jeremiah 23:7,8. At that point the nation of Israel, having endured a holocaust of tribulation, will have their eyes opened spiritually. They will understand Jesus as the Messiah! "Behold, He is coming with the clouds, and every eye will see Him, even those who pierced Him; and all the tribes of the earth will mourn over Him. Even so. Amen" (Revelation 1:7).

How thrilling it is to see Israel walking every day in the divine imprint that God has set for her!

7

Earth's Missing Multitude

◆ ══════════════════════ ◆

The Lord Himself will descend from heaven with a shout, with the voice of the archangel, and with the trumpet of God; and the dead in Christ shall rise first. Then we who are alive and remain shall be caught up together with them in the clouds to meet the Lord in the air, and thus we shall always be with the Lord.

—1 Thessalonians 4:16,17

One of my first speaking assignments as an evangelist for Kansas City Youth for Christ was an invitation to speak at a teen rally in Burlington, Iowa. My engagements up to that time had been local or in the states of Kansas or Missouri, near my hometown. I think I answered the letter the very day I received it. "Yes, I can come any way you want me, and every date is open for your selection" was my hurried, available reply.

The experience on this historic itinerant trip made its harrowing mark on me, indelibly remembered. And although many crowds have roared since hearing of the episode of that trip, it stills causes a slight tinge of fear.

I had been a Christian only a brief time and could have been labeled "the novice evangelist." Yet in the zeal of my newfound faith I wanted the world to know. Burlington Youth for Christ had an adult couple drive me from Kansas City to the small Iowa town. Shortly after the rally my brother Jeff and I were to be sent back to Kansas City via an Amtrack train sleeper coach.

I had numerous different travel habits back in those days. After talking all the way to Burlington, jabbering through dinner with the director and his wife, speaking, and dashing with Jeff to a departing train, I was exhausted.

Seated next to each other, within minutes Jeff and I were fast asleep. Maybe a coma was more accurate. I hadn't really noticed, but before Jeff nodded off he took off his coat, vest, tie, shoes, socks, and belt!

Farther down the track in the wee hours of the morning something abruptly woke me up. Disoriented and in a fatigued stupor, I turned suddenly to my left. There were Jeff's socks, shoes, tie, vest, and belt, but, *no Jeff.* "O God, Jesus must have come while I was sleeping, and I've been left behind," I said out loud. Springing to my feet, I raced to the diner car. He wasn't there. After I finished my investigation on every car on the train, even interrogating the conductor, I collapsed back in my now-uncomfortable train seat. A new, unlearned Christian, I was convinced Jesus had come. *I had been left behind!* Who would pick me up at the train station? Dad was supposed to, but if anyone was a Christian, he was. He would be gone for sure.

It sounds humorous now, but it was horrible then. I was freaked out. My mirrored image reflected back to me through the tint of the window as I stared unflinchingly at the darkened, lifeless, passing countryside. Even my familiar face seemed sinister, as if I were really a part of this emerging evil era.

What a relief when Jeff, just two seats in front of me (who wanted two seats to sleep in instead of just one), came and sat down next to my side. The sudden reality of not being left behind was a comfort still savored to this day! I rode on to Kansas City awake all the way until Dad's beaming face greeted me at the historic train station.

THE EVENT OF THE RAPTURE

The Bible prophesies a special moment in time when Jesus Christ will rapture His people from planet Earth. It may sound like a fairy tale, perhaps as much as Noah's predicted flood. Up to that time it had never rained. According to the Bible, God fed the greenery through dew. And here was old man Noah prophesying a torrential downpour because of man's sin!

The ancient Greeks specialized in philosophy. It was the Greeks who invented words to express precise and accurate thoughts. *Koine* greek, the original language of the New Testament, defined the meaning of words more than any other language in the world during the first century. The term *rapture* is a Latin word translated by the English words "caught up" in 1 Thessalonians 4:17. The Greek word is *harpazo* and means "caught up" or "caught away." Interestingly, it is the same Greek word that Paul used to describe his premature visit to heaven (2 Corinthians 12:3,4). The word points to a sudden, miraculous action and conveys a mystery type of transference, similar to Philip's unexplainable removal (cf. Acts 8:39).

Don't confuse the *rapture* with the *second coming* of Christ to planet Earth. In the rapture, Christ comes *for* His saints to receive them *to* Himself. In the second coming, Jesus Christ returns *to* the earth *with* His saints to judge the world (Revelation 19:11).

H.A. Ironside believed that the only mention of the rapture of Christians in the four Gospels was John 14:3: "If I go and prepare a place for you, I will come again and receive you to Myself, that where I am, there you may be also." I agree!

Paul says in 1 Corinthians 15:51 that we (Christians) shall not all sleep—a biblical term for death. In other words, not all of us are going to die physically. What is going to happen? We shall be changed! How? "In a moment, in the twinkling of an eye, at the last trumpet" replies verse 52. The twinkling of an eye has been defined by the Western Electric Corporation as $1/1000$ of a second. That is quick!

In an instantaneous moment we as Christians are going to be changed! The Greek word for changed is *allasso* and is used to indicate a total renewal or transformation. In a split moment Christ will return and we will be transformed into a glorified body and meet Him in the air!

Worldwide there is going to be a global evacuation of Christians from the earth at that divine moment. Talk about a news story—the rapture of Christians will rock news bureaus internationally like no other story in human history!

So what exactly is the rapture?

THE RAPTURE: A SURE EVENT

You can set your clock and calendar by God's prophetic Word. For every one promise about the first coming of Christ to the earth there are 20 promises about His second coming! In fact the very day Jesus died, 50 Old Testament prophecies were fulfilled! In the life, death, burial, resurrection, and ascension of Jesus, over 300 Old Testament prophecies were fulfilled. Think, however, of the ratio—

1 to 20. I have no doubt that if our Lord met all the conditions for His first coming, He won't be one second late for His second coming! It is a *sure* event. Count on it, and be ready for it.

"Now we request you, brethren, with regard to the coming of our Lord Jesus Christ, and our gathering together to Him" (2 Thessalonians 2:1). Here again is a sure reference to Christ's coming for His own. The term "gathering together" is *episunogogas* in the Greek. The word is normally a verb, but is used as a noun here to describe the Lord's gathering together of His redeemed at His coming.

Some have suggested that both 2 Timothy 4:1 and Titus 2:13 are also references to the preliminary rapture of the church before Christ's second return to the earth. Second Timothy 4:1 says, "I solemnly charge you in the presence of God and of Christ Jesus, who is to judge the living and the dead, and by His appearing and His kingdom." Titus 2:13, pointing first to the rapture, reads, "Looking for the blessed hope and the appearing of the glory of our great God and Savior, Christ Jesus."

Numerous reputable Bible teachers believe that the rapture is clearly pictured in Revelation 4:1: "After these things I looked, and behold, a door standing open in heaven, and the first voice which I had heard, like the sound of a trumpet speaking with me, said, Come up here, and I will show you what must take place after these things."

Later in Revelation 4 the 24 elders (we as Christians are pictured in these elders) will "fall down before Him who sits on the throne, and will worship Him who lives forever and ever, and will cast their crowns before the throne, saying, 'Worthy art Thou, our Lord and our God, to receive glory and honor and power'" (Revelation 4:10,11). Sounds identical to the judgment seat of Christ to me! (cf. 1 Corinthians

3:11-15; 2 Corinthians 5:10). (Keep in mind that the judgment seat of Christ can only occur *after* the rapture of the church.)

"The Lord Himself will descend..." (1 Thessalonians 4:16). Notice the dogma in this statement. Christ is coming! And He is coming for you and me. We need to stay happy!

Take a moment and read the exciting verses promising His return (1 Corinthians 1:7,8; 4:5; 1 Timothy 6:14; Hebrews 9:28; Colossians 3:4; Philippians 3:20). It is also notable that Paul referred to the second coming in every chapter of both of his letters to the church in the city of Thessalonica (1 Thessalonians 1:10; 2:19; 3:13; 4:16; 5:23; 2 Thessalonians 1:7,8; 2:1,2; 3:5).

THE RAPTURE: A SUDDEN EVENT

"The Lord Himself will descend from heaven with a shout, with the voice of the archangel and with the trumpet of God; and the dead in Christ shall rise first" (1 Thessalonians 4:16). What a striking way to say it! In the Greek, the word "shout" indicates a military command. We all know the response when the General walks into the room! Christ is coming from the heavenlies with a shout, and we will be raised to meet Him in the air.

Jesus is not going to touch His foot on this planet at the rapture. That momentous occasion will occur at His official second coming, when He is revealed to all the world (Revelation 19:11). Incidentally, at the strategic moment He returns, according to Zechariah chapter 9, He will rest His feet on the Mount of Olives and it will split in two.

But the rapture, the meeting of Christ in the air, will be sudden. This is exactly where "the twinkling of an eye" comes in. In $1/1000$ of a second we will be raised and changed!

Imagine what it will be like on the highways of the world's busiest cities when Christians vanish. Consider the airways... pilots, copilots, and flight attendants *gone!* Many business executives, factory workers, mothers, fathers, and young people will be *gone.*

What a nightmare! The common denominator with every missing person will be that each knew Jesus Christ as personal Lord and Savior.

It is my personal conviction that babies and small children, whether baptized or not, are unaccountable for their sins as far as God is concerned. Consequently, all will be taken at the rapture. (Some have suggested that the age of accountability is 12.)

Can you even begin to comprehend the grief and hysteria choking hospital nurseries and baby rooms everywhere? Every little one will be *gone.* Grieving parents will find no consolation. The evil day of retribution will have just been born.

Some will be surprised to not be taken. Jesus stated that some sincere individuals thinking themselves to be Christians will be speechless (read Matthew 22:9-14). It won't be just the overt unbeliever left behind. How many ministers will be left? Only God knows.

Acts 1:11 reminds us how Jesus left at His ascension and how He is coming at the rapture. Two angels said, "Men of Galilee, why do you stand looking into the sky? This Jesus, who has been taken up from you into heaven, will come in just the same way as you have watched Him go into heaven." Jesus departed *bodily*, He is returning *bodily*, and we will be raised *bodily* to meet Him in the air. The propulsion of our exit from earth's gravitational system will make NASA's Challenger seem like a turtle! I'm glad my name has been written in God's Book of Life. Is yours?

THE RAPTURE: A SUBLIME EVENT

"Then we who are alive and remain shall be caught up together with them in the clouds to meet the Lord in the air, and thus we shall always be with the Lord" (1 Thessalonians 4:17). What could be more enticing to every Christian than this ecstatic meeting with Christ in the air? Notice ... we who are *alive* and *remain* shall be caught up together with *them*. Who is that?

The rapture will mean a great reunion. When Christ returns to receive us to Himself, He is going to bring with Him all those believers who have previously died. This will be the reunion of all reunions, with Jesus orchestrating every detail. Imagine the hundreds of millions of people involved!

I will be able to reunite with Raymond Templeton on that day. Raymond went to high school with me, and he suffered from cystic fibrosis. I think he weighed only 65 pounds in our junior year, and that was his final year of suffering. Ruth, his mother (and the school librarian), was one of the finest Christians I have ever met. I used to stop by the library and see Ruth administering therapy on Raymond. He would be tilted, almost upside-down, inhaling a solution designed to break up the congestion in his lungs, and Ruth would be patting his back.

While he was under an oxygen tent at K.U. Medical Center we brought Raymond his class ring, but he got to wear it only a few days before his homegoing. When the doctors and his mom informed him that his death was certain, Raymond decided to plan the agenda of his funeral.

Every song he picked was one of triumph and rejoicing. For some reason he asked me to preach his funeral. When I walked into the little Crest Bible Church, Ruth greeted me just as the casket was slowly passing, destined for the front of the sanctuary. "Oh, Ruth, there's Raymond," I said automatically, pointing, my first time to see him since his death. "No, Jerry, that's not Raymond, that's the house he lived in," Ruth kindly corrected me. And that was the easiest funeral I ever spoke at, for I knew that Raymond was in heaven because he truly knew and loved the Lord.

Logged in my mind is Raymond and I on the bleachers of the smelly gymnasium after running a number of laps. I was breathing hard, trying to physically downshift. Raymond was gasping for air. I can still see his skeletally-inscribed rib cage embossed through his thin T-shirt, moving in and out. The coach made it clear that Raymond didn't have to participate, but Raymond didn't want any special concessions.

On that glorious day I will see Raymond, unhindered by any physical limitation.

The rapture will also mean the redemption of our bodies. John says it so succinctly: "Beloved, now we are children of God, and it has not appeared as yet what we shall be. We know that, when He appears, we shall be like Him, because we shall see Him just as He is" (1 John 3:2).

Our physical bodies will be transformed into glorified, heavenly bodies. Fatigue, memory loss, stress, and all other ailments will be forever over! "[He] will transform the body of our humble state into conformity with the body of His glory, by the exertion of the power that He has even to subject all things to Himself" (Philippians 3:21).

The longer I live, the more I understand the restrictions of my physical body. Although I travel nearly 200,000 miles a year (usually averaging 100 cities annually), I feel the stress more now than ever before. I used to stay up all night sometimes, and then work through the next day. My former practice was always to get the earliest flight out of whatever city I was in, so that I could always be back in my office by 11:00 A.M. My staff jokingly termed me "the android." They said, "Jerry's not human—people can't go that hard."

But now I have to go to bed at night! Man is complex; he is a physical, mental, emotional, and spiritual being. If one area is out of balance, we experience problems. But someday we will exchange this problem-laden body for a glorified body!

The rapture will mean preeminently the revelation of Jesus Christ. When John on the Island of Patmos turned to look at the glorified Christ, he said, "I fell at His feet as a dead man" (Revelation 1:17). Why? Because Christ was glorified. As mortals we don't fully understand this.

Listen to John's description of the glorified Christ: "I turned to see the voice that was speaking with me. And having turned I saw seven golden lampstands; and in the middle of the lampstands one like a son of man, clothed in a robe reaching to the feet, and girded across His breast with a golden girdle. And His head and His hair were white wool, like snow; and His eyes were like a flame of fire; and His feet were like burnished bronze, when it has been caused to glow in a furnace, and His voice was like the sound of many waters. And in His right hand He held seven stars; and out of His mouth came a sharp two-edged sword; and His face was like the sun shining in its strength" (Revelation 1:12-16).

At the rapture, Jesus Christ will be revealed to us in all His glory—and we will be like Him! So much could be said about Jesus, but I suppose in all the Bible I most cherish Luke 15:1: "Now all the tax-gatherers and the sinners were coming near Him to listen to Him." No one liked tax-gatherers. The unanimous opinion was that everyone hated them—everyone but Jesus. The high and mighty religious teachers repulsed the sinners. When Jesus came to town, Dr. Luke says that *all* of them went to hear Him.

Fanny Crosby, blind for life and the composer of many of the most spiritual songs in our hymnal, claimed that blindness was her blessing. One minister, while introducing Fanny for a brief word, commented to the congregation sympathetically about her visual limitation. Positioning her small frame behind the lectern, she replied, "Pastor, you shouldn't apologize that I am blind. I have the prospect that the first person I am going to see will be Jesus Christ!"

THE RAPTURE: A TRIPLE LOOK

When a person truly believes in the rapture it will produce three things in his or her life.

An upward look of expectation. When Jesus was alive He intimated to His apostles that He could have come in their lifetime: "You too be ready, for the Son of Man is coming at an hour that you do not expect" (Luke 12:40). "Therefore be on the alert—for you do not know when the master of the house is coming, whether in the evening, at midnight, at cockcrowing, or in the morning—lest he come suddenly and find you asleep" (Mark 13:35,36). "And if I go and prepare a place for you, I will come again and receive you to Myself" (John 14:3).

We ought to live every single day expecting the Lord to come. The late M.R. DeHaan popularized the phrase *perhaps today.* Dr. DeHaan emphasized that theme. D.J. DePree was one of the supporters of our ministry before his death late in 1990 at nearly 100 years of age. Christie and I got to know him very well. We ate lunch with him, fellowshiped with him, and prayed with him in his Michigan home. Mr. DePree was the former chairman of the board of Herman Miller Incorporated, one of the premier office manufacturing companies of the world. I remember seeing Mr. DePree on his knees praying. He would cry out to God complaining of his need for a greater burden for souls. Every single time we left his home, a holy impression was stamped on Christie and me. Mr. DePree makes me want to live with an attitude of expectation.

An inward look of purification. After reminding us that we will be transformed at the rapture like Jesus, John charges, "Everyone who has this hope fixed on Him purifies himself, just as He is pure" (1 John 3:3). The people who really believe in the coming of Christ are those who are living pure lives. There is no greater virtue than the power of personal purity.

Shortly after I married Christie she taught me clearly that I don't ever invite anyone to our home without giving her ample warning. Why? Because she wants everything perfectly clean before a visitor comes in. If we truly believe that Christ is coming, we will clean out the residue of disobedience in our lives.

An outward look of occupation. In Luke 19:13 Jesus said, "Occupy until I come" (KJV). The mode of every Christian should be to work as hard as possible for Christ until He comes. We need to win as many people to Christ as possible.

Some churches I go to are like a morgue. The lights are low and dim, the sound is horrible, and the people are unexcited. No wonder young people flock to the rock concert instead! It's time to get busy, to get inventive in sharing the redemptive message of Jesus.

Christ is going to return! What about your neighbor or family member? Have you told them about Jesus and His way to salvation and heaven? What about the person you work with or attend school with? Do they know that Jesus

Christ is going to return? "How then shall they call upon Him in whom they have not believed? And how shall they believe in Him whom they have not heard? And how shall they hear without a preacher?" (Romans 10:14,15).

Will you be that preacher?

8

Unlocking Daniel's Precise Predictions

✦ ══════════════════════════════════ ✦

When you see the abomination of desolation which was spoken of through Daniel the prophet, standing in the holy place, let the reader understand.

—Matthew 24:15

Many people simply do not understand the most pivotal, strategic book in the Bible on end-times prophecy. It is impossible to understand the last New Testament book, the Revelation, apart from a thorough knowledge of Daniel's 12 informative chapters. The 356 verses in this classic book should have the complete attention of every Christian.

Daniel is the key which opens the door to the panorama of prophetic Scripture. Jesus stamps His endorsement on Daniel's book of truth, though He cautions, "Let the reader understand." There is no reason for this book to be a quandary to any believer in Jesus Christ who is eager to comprehend God's precise prediction of future events.

THE TIME AND SETTING

In exact fulfillment of the prophet Jeremiah's warning, the disobedient Jewish Israelites had became "displaced persons." Their ceaseless sinning and defiance of God's law had to be punished: "This whole land shall be a desolation and a horror, and these nations shall serve the king of Babylon seventy years" (Jeremiah 25:11).

The prophetic judgment included not only Judah but her neighbors. This period of exile was from 605 B.C. to 538 B.C., roughly seventy years. "In the first year of his reign I, Daniel, observed in the books the number of the years which was revealed as the word of the Lord to Jeremiah the prophet for the completion of the desolations of Jerusalem, namely, seventy years" (Daniel 9:2).

As God used Pharaoh to accomplish His sovereign will in exodus days, likewise the Lord used Nebuchadnezzar, the king of the infamous and pagan Babylon, to conquer Jerusalem, destroy the temple, and return with hostages. In 605 B.C. events changed dramatically for the Israelites and Jerusalem. In this first move of conquest, Daniel and his three friends, Hananiah, Mishael, and Azariah, were relocated into a city which had no reverence for Israel's God.

A few years later, in 597 B.C., rebellious Judean kings Jehoiakim and Jehoiachin further provoked Nebuchadnezzar to cause Jerusalem to buckle. The godless king evacuated 10,000 captives, including Jehoiachin and the young prophet Ezekiel. (Read Ezekiel 1:1-3; 2 Chronicles 36:10; 2 Kings 24:8-20.)

But this wasn't enough. In 587 B.C., after a lengthy siege, Nebuchadnezzar plundered Jerusalem, destroyed the temple, and extinguished the entire Jewish community. (Read 2 Kings 25:1-7; Jeremiah 34:1-7; 39:1-7; 52:1-11.)

The events in Daniel cover approximately 70 years, from 605 B.C. to 536 B.C. John Walvoord suggests that Daniel may have lived on to about 530 B.C., perhaps exceeding 70 or 75 years of age, and probably penned the book in the last decade of his life under the inspiration of the Holy Spirit.

There is no question that Daniel was the author. "But as for you, Daniel, conceal these words and seal up the book until the end of time; many will go back and forth, and knowledge will increase" (Daniel 12:4; note 7:2,15,28; 8:1,15,27; 9:2,22; 10:2,7,11,12; 12:5). The prophet Ezekiel in prophetic vision established Daniel's rank of faith (Ezekiel 14:14,20; 28:3). This was given after Daniel had assumed a leadership position in Nebuchadnezzar's Babylonian court.

As nearly every Bible scholar has pointed out, the book of Daniel is written in two different languages: Hebrew and Aramaic. Critics have had a field day with this. The division is 1:1–2:3, Hebrew; 2:4–7:28, Aramaic; 8:1–12:13, Hebrew Biblical Aramaic, in this context, could also be called Syriac or Chaldee. It was the common language of the Gentiles at the time. Quite simply, the best response to the critics is that the use of Aramaic, which was the lingua franca of the period, was material which concerned the *Gentile world* rather than *Jewish Israel*. Consequently the Aramaic language was used.

DANIEL: APOCALYPTIC LITERATURE

The word "apocalypse" comes from a Greek word which means "unveiling" or "revelation." Though all of the Bible could loosely fall under this category of thought, in the strictest sense Daniel is the only Old Testament book of apocalypse. Correspondingly, Revelation is the only New Testament book that is explicitly apocalyptic. The heart of apocalyptic literature is predictive prophecy which employs two main ingredients: *visions* and *symbols* (vehicles of revelations). The thrust of apocalyptic literature has theological content which is primarily with an end-times focus.

Because of the difficulty in properly interpreting this style of writing, interpretive error is common. In fact, there are no special hermeneutical (Bible interpretation) rules designed for apocalyptic literature. Outside of Scripture apocalyptic literature abounds. But these writings are theologically insignificant and bear no mark whatsoever of divine inspiration or infallibility. Daniel, however, is one of the grandest examples of divinely inspired apocalyptic literature. A Bible student must be careful to decipher accurately what are the prophetic elements indicated. One essential hermeneutical rule is *Scripture interprets Scripture.*

The purpose of predictive apocalyptic writings is to reveal the culture and times hundreds of years in advance of their actual occurrence. Imagine John, on the Island of Patmos, seeing the events of the tribulation, man's technologically advanced society nearly 20 centuries later; it must have been mind-boggling! Apocalyptic literature is like stepping on a rapidly circling merry-go-round: If you aren't careful, and keep your eyes fixed, you have to jump off with dizziness.

Many Christians and fine ministers have simply ignored these areas of the Bible. Yet we can carefully discern what God is saying with each vision and symbol in apocalyptic literature.

THE EVIL CITY OF BABYLON

Because of their idolatry, the Israelites were carried off as prisoners to the world center of idolatry, Babylon. Babylon was one of the most wicked cities of the ancient world. Notably, after this captivity the Israelites never had a problem with idolatry again.

Near the rubble of present-day Baghdad, after the Iraq War of 1991, lie the ruins of Babylon (30 miles southwest of

Baghdad). As has been widely reported, Saddam Hussein has viewed himself as something of a contemporary Nebuchadnezzar. Bible Professor Charles Dyer, in his 1991 book, *Rise of Babylon*, reports that Saddam Hussein is attempting to rebuild Babylon.

> As of February 1990, over sixty thousand bricks had been laid in the reconstruction of Nebuchadnezzar's fabled city. Saddam Hussein has ignored the objections of archaeologists who consider it a crime to build over ancient ruins. On the exact site of ancient Babylon, he has reconstructed the Southern Palace of Nebuchadnezzar, including the Procession Street, a Greek theatre, many temples, what was once Nebuchadnezzar's throne room, and a half-scale model of the Ishtar Gate. Hussein plans to rebuild the hanging gardens, once considered one of the seven wonders of the world: he has offered a 1.5 million prize to any Iraqi who can devise a plan to irrigate the gardens using only the technology available in ancient Babylon.[1]

It is interesting to note that the birth of mankind originated near Babylon. The Bible mentions Babylon over 280 times, and many occurrences have a future significance. Zechariah was born in Babylon during the captivity and returned to Jerusalem in 538 B.C.

For nearly 2000 years Babylon was the most important city in the world. It must have been built some time before 2300 B.C. Genesis 10:10 cites Babel (Babylon) as part of the empire of Nimrod. Nebuchadnezzar was Babylon's greatest king; he enlarged the city to an area of six square miles and beautified it with magnificent buildings. The city had massive double walls encircling it, with 18 major gates set into the walls. There were scores of pagan temples in the city, including one to the patron god Marduk, flanked by a ziggurat or temple tower. Also there was a pagan, religiously sacred, processional way from the main gate, the Ishtar Gate. Bordering the gate and the walls facing the way were colored and decorated enamel bricks painted with lions, dragons, and bulls.

Located between the Tigris and Euphrates rivers, Babylon stood in defiance to everything that God represented. Babylonia was the term for the region representing the ancient pagan empire between the Tigris and Euphrates in southern Mesopotamia. It was a long, narrow country about 40 miles at its widest point, representing an area of about 8000 square miles. It is interesting to know that the Garden of Eden, man's original utopia home, was located near the Euphrates River. Early civilization fanned out from this location. Whereas Jerusalem typifies the city of God, Babylon typifies the city of Satan.

It was in this evil city that Daniel was relocated. King Nebuchadnezzar attempted to conform Daniel to the pagan system: "He ordered him to teach them the literature and language of the Chaldeans. And the king appointed for them a daily ration from the king's choice food and from the wine which he drank, and appointed that they should be educated three years, at the end of which they were to enter the king's personal service" (Daniel 1:4,5).

King Nebuchadnezzar, an enthusiast of the Babylonian system, tried diligently to change Daniel dietetically, societally, academically, socially, and religiously.

It was because the Chaldeans were experts in magic lore that the term "Chaldean" occurs alongside magicians, enchanters and sorcerers in Daniel 2:2. This was the art for which they became famous and to which they gave their name. The accumulated literature included omens, magic incantations, prayers and hymns, myths and legends, and scientific formulae for skills such as glass-making, mathematics and astrology. To begin to study Babylonian literature was to enter a completely alien thought-world. According to the Sumerians and Babylonians, two classes of persons inhabited the universe: the human race and the gods. Preeminence belonged to the gods, though they were not all equal. At the lower end of the divine scale came a host of minor deities and demons, while a trinity of great gods, Anu, Enlil, Ea, stood at their head.[2]

The Old Testament prophets Isaiah and Jeremiah predicted the downfall of the city of Babylon. According to their prophecies this would happen not only because of sin, but because Babylon destroyed Jerusalem, God's chosen city, and deported His people, the Israelites. (Notice Isaiah 14:22; 21:9; 43:14; Jeremiah 50:9; 51:37.) The ruins of Babylon, once the proud capital city of a mighty empire, are viewed today as a reminder that God's Word is true!

DANIEL'S GOLDEN CHARACTER

"But Daniel made up his mind that he would not defile himself with the king's choice food or with the wine which he drank; so he sought permission from the commander of the officials that he might not defile himself" (Daniel 1:8). This has to be one of the most beautiful expressions of commitment to God in the entire Bible. Daniel made up his mind! This is why so many Christians today accomplish so little for their Lord—they have not "made up their mind." Everything was dictating for Daniel to conform. Had he wanted to ascend Nebuchadnezzar's promotion ladder, all

Daniel had to do was conform. But to Daniel that was an impossibility!

This great servant of God was a vessel who was usable. God could impart to him a dynamic look into the far future because the Lord saw genuine spiritual character in Daniel. One Bible teacher has suggested that with the exception of Moses and Solomon, Daniel was the most learned man in the Old Testament. Perhaps he was also the most thoroughly trained for his critical role in prophetic history and apocalyptic literature.

We do not know Daniel's exact age when he was deported to Babylon and the attempted reprogramming began. Several scholars agree that Daniel and his devoted Jewish friends were probably in their teens. This only accentuates his fidelity and godly character. As a young, impressionable man, Nebuchadnezzar's polytheistic, material-laden city meant nothing to him; Daniel's allegiance was to Jehovah alone. It is my prayer that God will raise up a Daniel-generation in these closing days of the church age. Kids today are so peer-conscious; the temptation is to be reticent to stand up to friends. As a teenager, Daniel was *God*-conscious. Serving the Lord was the first priority of his life!

One of the major criticisms from an unbelieving world today is the moral failure of many of the supposed representatives and messengers of Jesus Christ. The term "televangelist" is almost a term of contempt in the secular marketplace of our day. But notice the difference in Daniel's influence on an occultic-oriented king: "Then the commissioners and satraps began trying to find a ground of accusation against Daniel in regard to government affairs; but they could find no ground of accusation or evidence of corruption, inasmuch as he was faithful, and no negligence or corruption was to be found in him" (Daniel 6:4). Daniel cut no corners nor selfishly manipulated his exalted position.

In spite of King Darius' decree, Daniel continued to pray. Three times a day, kneeling and facing Jerusalem, in gratitude he petitioned God. This later led Darius to observe "...your God whom you constantly serve" (Daniel 6:16). Darius acknowledged Daniel as a "servant of the living God" (6:20). Nebuchadnezzar may have been converted through Daniel's holy life. Darius also sounded like a preacher in Daniel 6:26,27, after Daniel survived the lion's den. Perhaps he too became a believer. There is nothing more influentially powerful than a believer's godly life!

THE TWO HALVES OF DANIEL

Israel as a nation was at a bleak period when God inspired the book of Daniel. It had a contemporary message for the Jewish people and a futurist blueprint for the end of the age. Daniel speaks to both the Gentile and Jewish people in its prophetic utterance. Similar to Esther, the book of Daniel reveals God's continued work with His people in spite of their chastisement brought on by sin. It is interesting to note that Daniel gives little information about the Jewish captives in Babylon or history of the Israelite nation. Only a few episodes in Daniel's long life are even mentioned. The book does not tell us how, when, or where Daniel died.

Many feel that it is impossible to understand what has been termed the Olivet Discourse (Jesus' prophetic sermon delivered when He was seated on the Mount of Olives in Matthew chapters 24 and 25) without understanding Daniel's prophetic message.

The book of Daniel divides into two halves. The first half, chapters 1–6 is historical; the second half, chapters 7–12, is apocalyptic or prophetic.

Daniel's focus is not primarily on the *first* coming of Jesus Christ; chapters 7 and 12 sketch vivid details of Christ's *second* coming. The first coming of Jesus is suggested, however, in Daniel 9:26: "After the sixty-two weeks the Messiah will be cut off and have nothing, and the people of the prince who is to come will destroy the city and the sanctuary."

> It is agreed by almost all evangelical interpreters that these two events, the cutting off of the Messiah (Anointed One) and the destruction of the sanctuary, refer to the crucifixion of Christ and the destruction of Jerusalem by the Romans. These two events were separated by a period of nearly forty years (29-70 A.D.). Yet, in the literary order of the passage, they are both after the sixty-ninth week and before the final "one week" mentioned in the next verse.[3]

PREDICTION 1:
FUTURE GENTILE
MILITARY POWERS

As has been repeatedly stressed by nearly every expository book on Daniel, this book provides the clearest record of the history of man from Daniel's day to the second coming of Christ. When Daniel was alive, Nebuchadnezzar and Babylon were the dominant military controlling powers of the day.

However, in visions from God in chapters 2 and 7, Daniel

accurately predicted the future military powers from his day until the second coming of Christ. Even secular historians now confirm that Daniel's predictions were absolutely accurate. Equally amazing is the fact that the future military powers were first prophesied through a dream of Nebuchadnezzar (2:1-45) and again predicted in exact harmony with a later dream and vision of Daniel himself (7:1-28). These two chapters reinforce each other's predictions of the future military powers that would come into existence and domination.

Responding to Nebuchadnezzar, Daniel interpreted the puzzling dream (2:31-45) for the king. Subsequently he was promoted to an influential position (2:48). Daniel underscored to the king that it was *God* who revealed the dream (2:19-23,27,28) for a sovereign purpose. The purpose was abundantly clear: "The great God has made known to the king what will take place in the future; so the dream is true, and its interpretation is trustworthy" (2:45).

There were four different dominant military powers destined to control the world.

Babylon—the first kingdom. To explain the representation of the military kingdoms succinctly, Nebuchadnezzar's dream pictured a statue of extraordinary splendor (2:31). The body of the grand statue represented the future. The gold head represented Nebuchadnezzar as a world dictator, or emperor, and Babylon's power itself (2:32). Daniel stated "You, O king, are the king of kings, to whom the God of heaven has given the kingdoms, the power, the strength, and the glory; and wherever the sons of men dwell, or the beast of the field, or the birds of the sky, He has given them into your hand and has caused you to rule over them all. You are the head of gold" (2:37,38).

Medo-Persia—the second kingdom. "Its breast and its arms [were] of silver..." (Daniel 2:32). Daniel interprets, "After you there will rise another kingdom inferior to you" (2:39). History documents the fact that the Persian ruler Cyrus conquered Babylon in less than a month. Due to its power, Persia swallowed up the Medes and became one dominant force. Chapter 6 affirms this conglomeration (see 6:8, 12,15). The two equal horns of the ram are identified as "the kings of Media and Persia" (8:20).

This kingdom, beginning in Daniel's day, survived and ruled for over 200 years, until the time of Alexander the Great, 336 B.C.

Greece—the third kingdom. "Its belly and its thighs [were] of bronze..." (Daniel 2:32). Interpretation: "Then another third kingdom of bronze [will arise], which will rule over all the earth" (2:39). From Macedonia to Africa, history details the marvel of the 30-year-old legend, Alexander the Great, who conquered the civilized world around the Mediterranean. His kingdom tentacles even stretched into India.

Rome—the fourth kingdom. "Its feet [were] partly of iron and partly of clay" (Daniel 2:33). The prophecy continues, "There will be a fourth kingdom as strong as iron; inasmuch as iron crushes and shatters all things, so, like iron that breaks in pieces, it will crush and break all these in pieces" (2:40). Born into existence in 241 B.C., the Roman empire did precisely what Daniel described. Every nation standing in the way of world domination was broken in pieces. Of all the four metals mentioned, iron is the strongest. The saying was, "The sun never sets on the Roman empire." Rome's control extended to southern Britain, France, Belgium, Switzerland, Germany, and beyond. Jesus Christ was born into a world controlled by Rome's iron fist.

By contrast, the Roman empire was ruthless in its destruction of civilizations and peoples, killing captives by the thousands and selling them into slavery by the hundreds of thousands. Rome could never get enough of conquest. Rome had no interest in raising conquered nations to any high level of development; all her designs were imperial: Let the nations be crushed and stamped under foot.[4]

Out of Rome came several different countries which exist even today. These countries are represented by the ten horns: "After this I kept looking in the night visions, and behold, a fourth beast, dreadful and terrifying and extremely strong; and it had large iron teeth. It devoured and crushed, and trampled down the remainder with its feet; and it was different from all the beasts that were before it, and it had ten horns" (7:7). The kingdoms formed out of the Roman empire are still in existence today in the form of various European countries. Boundary lines have changed, but these fragments of the Roman empire still exist in our time.

Jesus Christ's eternal reign—the fifth kingdom. As mighty as Rome was, and as strong as the nations are today, the Bible predicts emphatically that Christ will return to the earth to reign. We are not going to reign with Christ on Mars or in some ethereal world. We are going to reign with Christ *on this planet*!

Rehearsing Nebuchadnezzar's dream to him, Daniel says, "You continued looking until a stone was cut out without hands, and it struck the statue on its feet of iron and clay, and crushed them. Then the iron, the clay, the bronze, the silver and the gold were crushed all at the same time, and became like chaff from the summer threshing floors; and the wind carried them away so that not a trace of them was found. But the stone that struck the statue became a great mountain and filled the whole earth" (2:34,35).

Daniel gives the interpretation: "In the days of those kings the God of heaven will set up a kingdom which will never be destroyed, and that kingdom will not be left for another people; it will crush and put an end to all these kingdoms, but it will itself endure forever" (2:44).

Jesus Christ will return physically to this earth to set up His eternal kingdom. Only those who know Christ personally are going to be residents in this all-conquering kingdom.

Daniel's vision in chapter 7 perfectly coordinates with Nebuchadnezzar's dream of chapter 2. Although chapter 7 appears after chapter 5 (Belshazzar's drunken orgy, which resulted in his death and loss of the kingdom), the time of Daniel's dream occurred 14 years before the fall of Babylon, 553 B.C. (Nebuchadnezzar died in 562 B.C.) Chapter 7, Daniel's dream, took place between chapters 4 and 5. So as not to be too lengthy, let me summarize the symbols and interpretation of chapter 7. Daniel's dream is far more detailed and lengthy in chapter 7 than was Nebuchadnezzar's vision of chapter 2.

"Four great beasts were coming up from the sea, different from one another. The first was like a lion and had the wings of an eagle. I kept looking until its wings were plucked, and it was lifted up from the ground and made to stand on two feet like a man; a human mind also was given to it" (7:3,4). This is obviously Babylon, the first kingdom. The lion made to stand upon his feet as a man, and with a man's heart given to it, represents God's humbling of Nebuchadnezzar described in chapter 4.

"And behold, another beast, a second one, resembling a bear. And it was raised up on one side, and three ribs were in its mouth between its teeth; and thus they said to it, 'Arise, devour much meat!' " (7:5). This is the Medo-Persian empire. The three ribs in its mouth may represent the three greatest conquests this kingdom achieved.

"After this I kept looking, and behold, another one, like a leopard, which had on its back four wings of a bird; the beast also had four heads, and dominion was given to it" (7:6). This is the empire of Greece. The leopard signifies the rapidity with which Alexander the Great conquered and spread his world dominance.

As has been stated already, 7:7 refers to the Roman empire, the fourth kingdom.

Gloriously, the fifth kingdom is Christ's eternal reign: "I kept looking until thrones were set up, and the Ancient of Days took His seat; His vesture was like white snow, and the hair of His head like pure wool. His throne was ablaze with flames, its wheels were a burning fire. A river of fire was flowing and coming out from before Him; thousands upon thousands were attending Him, and myriads upon myriads were standing before Him; the court sat, and the books were opened" (7:9,10).

Imagine this wondrous kingdom of Jesus Christ! Nothing can compare to it: "To Him was given dominion, glory and a kingdom, that all the peoples, nations, and men of every language might serve Him. His dominion is an everlasting dominion which will not pass away, and His kingdom is one which will not be destroyed" (7:14).

Incidentally, the Ancient of Days refers to God the Father. Jesus will renovate the earth at His coming, and He shall reign.

PREDICTION 2:
ANTICHRIST CLEARLY DISPLAYED

Daniel speaks repeatedly of the Antichrist, the coming satanic ruler. He will reign on the earth, but only for a temporary time. Daniel tells us from where the Antichrist will arise: "As for the ten horns [nations], out of this kingdom ten kings will arise; and another will arise after them, and he will be different from the previous ones and will subdue three kings" (7:24). Dr. John Whitcomb reasons that this verse is describing the Antichrist's first half of the "seventieth week." Simply put, this is the Antichrist emerging in his first 3½ years of the tribulation.

The Antichrist will rise to power by his conquest of three kings (nations). The tenfold confederacy will launch him into his future domination orbit. He will be different, or diverse, from the other ten nation rulers. Why? Because he will be guided craftily by Satan (see 2 Thessalonians 2:4).

"While I was contemplating the horns, behold, another horn, a little one, came up among them, and three of the first horns were pulled out by the roots before it; and behold, this horn possessed eyes like the eyes of a man, and a mouth uttering great boasts" (7:8). Make no mistake—the Antichrist will be a mortal. But he will be hyped up with demonic ingenuity. Revelation 13 with its many masculine pronouns reminds us the Antichrist is a *man*.

Satan's man will have the gift of gab. He will be an orator par excellence, much greater than the mesmerizing Hitler was. This man who "utters great boasts" will sway the masses.

"... and the meaning of the ten horns that were on its head, and the other horn which came up, and before which the three of them fell, namely, that horn which had eyes and a mouth uttering great boasts, and which was larger in appearance than its associates" (7:20). The Antichrist is even a physical Casanova; the disguised evil one is handsome. He has the admiration and infatuation of everyone. He stands head-and-shoulders above the rest.

"And he will speak out against the Most High and wear down the saints of the Highest One, and he will attempt to make alterations in times and in law; and they will be given into his hand for a time, times, and half a time" (7:25). This verse obviously describes the Antichrist's last 3½-year reign of terror. Notice his extermination plan:

1. Defiantly he will blaspheme the God of heaven. At this point he will insist that he be worshiped (Revelation 13:8). "And there was given to him a mouth speaking arrogant words and blasphemies" (13:5).

2. Mr. Antichrist will change or "alter" the previous religious system. This is, of course, when he breaks his covenant with the Jewish people and disallows temple worship (cf. Daniel 9:27).

3. His duration is identified as a time, times, and half a time. What does this mean? The angel later responds to Daniel, "I heard the man dressed in linen, who was above the waters of the river, as he raised his right hand and his left toward heaven, and swore by Him who lives forever that it would be for a time, times, and half a time; and as soon as they finished shattering the power of the holy people, all these events will be completed" (Daniel 12:7). Referencing 4:25, a "time" signifies a year. This period means, undoubtedly, 3½ years or 42 months. (Read Revelation 11:2 and 13:5.)

4. He will wear down the saints of the Most High. "I kept looking, and that horn was waging war with

the saints and overpowering them" (7:21). (See also Revelation 13:7.) The scourge of the Antichrist will be awesome for Israelites during the final 3½ years of the tribulation. The 144,000 evangelists will be Divinely protected from death. But they will suffer (Matthew 25:35-40). Other Jews will flee to secret areas for protection (Revelation 12:13-16). You can rest assured that they will be longing for the Messiah to come in that day. In a sense, the hatred of Adolf Hitler, magnified hundreds of times, will be unleashed upon God's chosen people by Satan's superman.

As has been stated in the chapter on the Antichrist, the Antichrist will make a covenant with the Jews during the tribulation (Daniel 9:27). Later this covenant will be broken and horror will begin.

"Then after the sixty-two weeks the Messiah will be cut off and have nothing, and the people of the prince who is to come will destroy the city and the sanctuary" (Daniel 9:26). The amazing peacemaker will stop all temple worship. The Jews will shriek at what will happen to their holy city, Jerusalem. This is where Revelation 11:2 fits in: "And leave out the court which is outside the temple, and do not measure it, for it has been given to the nations; and they will tread under foot the holy city for forty-two months."

The other portion in Daniel spotlighting the Antichrist is 11:36-39: "The king will do as he pleases, and he will exalt and magnify himself above every god, and will speak monstrous things against the God of gods; and he will prosper until the indignation is finished; for that which is decreed will be done. And he will show no regard for the gods of his fathers or for the desire of women, nor will he show regard for any other god; for he will magnify himself above them all. But instead he will honor a god of fortresses, a god whom his fathers did not know; he will honor him with gold, silver, costly stones, and treasures. And he will take action against the strongest of fortresses with the help of a foreign god; he will give great honor to those who acknowledge him, and he will cause them to rule over the many, and will parcel out land for a price."

This text fits the other predictive passages for the Antichrist in his last 3¹/₂-year demonic fit (2 Thessalonians 2:4; Revelation 13 and 17). Prior to verse 36 the prophecy concerned itself with the Persian and Greece Empires. But now there is a break. Daniel, guided by the Holy Spirit, focuses on the Antichrist.

Many people hold the belief that the Antichrist will be a Jew. This is deduced from the statement, "He will show no regard for the gods of his fathers" (11:36). Correlating to this thought is that the Jewish people will not accept, align with, or subordinate themselves to even a charismatic world ruler unless he is a Jew. The King James Version reads, "Neither shall he regard the God of his fathers...." This is a Jewish phrase. To espouse the claim that he is a contemporary Messiah and have millions of people believe it, he must be a Jew. Revelation 13 sees the beast coming up out of the sea, symbolizing a Gentile nation. But the Antichrist could be a Jew born and raised in a Gentile nation.

But let us never forget that the Antichrist's doom is sure. God will prevail even when earth seems in its darkest, most evil hour. Daniel makes this very clear: "But the court will sit for judgment, and his dominion will be taken away, annihilated and destroyed forever" (7:26).

PREDICTION 3:
THE COMING TRIBULATION

"And there will be a time of distress such as never oc-curred since there was a nation until that time; and at that time your people, everyone who is found written in the book, will be rescued" (Daniel 12:1). Daniel pulls back the curtains to reveal the horrors of the tribulation. This verse corresponds to the events in Revelation chapters 6 to 19, where the vials, plagues, and wrath of God are unleashed on an unbelieving society.

PREDICTION 4:
THE RETURN OF JESUS CHRIST

"I kept looking in the night visions, and behold, with the clouds of heaven one like a Son of Man was coming, and He came up to the Ancient of Days and was presented before Him" (7:13). What a marvelous picture! Here we see God the Father, the Ancient of Days, receiving the Son of Man, Jesus Christ.

Christ is going to return and be the Victor!

PREDICTION 5:
THE FUTURE KINGDOM OF JESUS CHRIST

Daniel as a book strongly establishes the millennial reign of Jesus Christ. When Christ returns He is going to estab-lish His kingdom here on this earth. It will be a totally different earth from the one we have known. Not only will there be no pollution, no evil, and no unrest, but there will also be no sin.

Imagine a world where sin and all its calamities are forever erased! This is the future kingdom of Jesus Christ.

For one thousand years we are going to reign right here on this planet. God will remodel earth, and it will radiate with His perfection.

"But the saints of the Highest One will receive the kingdom and possess the kingdom forever, for all ages to come" (7:18). Again, "Until the Ancient of Days came, and judgment was passed in favor of the saints of the Highest One, and the time arrived when the saints took possession of the kingdom" (7:22). Daniel wanted to make this point completely clear. "Then the sovereignty, the dominion, and the greatness of all the kingdoms under the whole heaven will be given to the people of the saints of the Highest One; His kingdom will be an everlasting kingdom, and all the dominions will serve and obey Him" (7:27). This is stated in 7:14 also.

There could be no better kingdom than our Lord's, and it is coming!

PREDICTION 6:
THE TEN-NATION CONFEDERACY

The fourth prophesied beast, the Roman empire, was "different from all the beasts that were before it, and it had ten horns" (Daniel 7:7). Verse 8 says, "While I was contemplating the horns, behold, another horn, a little one, came up among them...." Daniel continues, "Then I desired to know the exact meaning of the fourth beast...and the meaning of the ten horns that were on its head" (7:19,20).

The angel responded, "As for the ten horns, out of this kingdom ten kings will arise..." (7:24).

Much has been written and stated about the United States of Europe, and that developing body certainly fits here.

Some economists and world-watchers strongly believe that unified Europe will become a dominant—perhaps *the* dominant—player in the next several years. Possibly a decade from now, if Jesus tarries, the boom will not be in Japan or America but in Europe.

Out of the ten horns comes the little horn. Out of this confederacy comes the Antichrist. Where is he now? Only God knows. Probably ascending the political ladder somewhere in Europe.

PREDICTION 7:
KNOWLEDGE INCREASED, TRAVEL SPEEDED UP

Although the reference is quite brief, it bears recognition and highlighting: "But as for you, Daniel, conceal these words and seal up the book until the end of time; many will go back and forth, and knowledge will increase" (12:4).

More scientists and prolific minds are alive today than ever before in the history of man. My children are being educated in a school district which registers among the top ten in the nation. It never ceases to amaze me how much more my kids know than I did as a child. Generationally, knowledge has been and is increasing just as Daniel's vision revealed.

In a few years our present system of travel will seem archaic. Anyone who reads *Time, Newsweek*, or *U.S. News & World Report*, and is involved in business, is globally oriented. Capitalism and the free-enterprise system enjoy their richest rewards in a global community. Yet when Daniel penned these words, the fastest mode of transportation was a horse, or a chariot pulled by one!

PREDICTION 8:
THE BATTLE DURING THE TRIBULATION

Not to be mistaken with the final battle of Armageddon, Daniel sees a battle coming against the Antichrist from the kings of the North and South.

"And at the end time the king of the South will collide with him, and the king of the North will storm against him with chariots, with horsemen, and with many ships; and he will enter countries, overflow them, and pass through" (11:40). The antecedent "him," used twice in this verse, must refer to the Antichrist.

"He will also enter the Beautiful Land, and many countries will fall; but these will be rescued out of his hand..." (11:41).

"Then he will stretch out his hand against other countries, and the land of Egypt will not escape. But he will gain control over the hidden treasures of gold and silver, and over the precious things of Egypt; and Libyans and Ethiopians will follow at his heels. But rumors from the East and from the North will disturb him, and he will go forth with great wrath to destroy and annihilate many. And he will pitch the tents of his royal pavilion between the seas and the beautiful Holy Mountain; yet he will come to his end, and no one will help him" (11:42-45).

The king of the North seems to be Russia. Russia is a vast geographic, military power. Ezekiel chapters 38 and 39 prophecy that Russia will come down on Israel in a battle confrontation during the tribulation. Perhaps what evokes Russia's attack and fear is when the Antichrist breaks his covenant relationship with Israel, proclaims himself god, demands to be worshiped, and issues his mark—and Russia feels threatened. This would place the battle at the midpoint of the tribulation period.

The king of the South would seem to be an Egyptian force or aligned forces. The question has been raised as to whether the "he's" of verses 41-43 are the Antichrist or a reference to one of the kings in conflict. Most premillennialists relate these references to the Antichrist.

The countries he sweeps through (verse 41) are those aligned in his ten-horn confederation. This battle will extend over a period of time. In verse 44, the king of the East which "disturbs him" must be the 200-million-plus Chinese army. This corresponds to Revelation 9:13-21. The number of the army indicated in this passage is 200,000,000 soldiers. That is exactly the size of the Chinese army today!

The king of the North remounts for another attack (verse 44). Many will die, according to verse 44.

Now we come to the time of his end (verse 45). As the major armies of the world come into a full-scale conflagration, Jesus Christ returns to this planet. This is majestically stated in Revelation 19:17-21. Their guns pointed at one another will be redirected at our Lord. The Commander-in-Chief of the heavenly forces will instantly conquer the forces of the world.

Daniel is mentally and physically exhausted by everything he has seen. "At this point the revelation ended. As for me, Daniel, my thoughts were greatly alarming me and my face grew pale, but I kept the matter to myself" (7:28).

Standing next to the interpretive angel, Daniel poses a question that every Christian should be asking: "My Lord, what will be the outcome of these events?" (12:8). The angel's answer: "Many will be purged, purified and refined; but the wicked will act wickedly, and none of the wicked will understand, but those who have insight will understand" (12:10).

Let's pray that God will give us insight so that we will truly understand!

9

Satan's Superman

✦ ══════════════════ ✦

Then that lawless one will be revealed whom the Lord will slay with the breath of His mouth and bring to an end by the appearance of His coming; that is, the one whose coming is in accord with the activity of Satan, with all the power and signs and false wonders, and with all the deception of wickedness for those who perish, because they did not receive the love of the truth so as to be saved.

—2 Thessalonians 2:8-10

Historian Arnold Toynbee once said, "The nations are now ready to give the kingdoms of the world to any one man who will offer us a solution to our world's problems."

Paul-Henri Spaak, one of the early planners of the European Common Market (and former General Secretary of Nato), said, "We do not want another committee, we have too many already. What we want is a man of sufficient stature to hold the allegiance of all the people and to lift us up out of the economic morass to which we are sinking.

Send us such a man, and be he God or be he the Devil, we will receive him."

As the various nations of the world face enormous political, economic, societal, and moral problems, many people are looking for a man to come on the horizon—a man with a worldwide game plan for unity and international harmony. They do not care if it is God or Satan—they just want someone to solve their cataclysmic problems.

Eric Blair in the year 1949 wrote the novel *1984* and coined the expression "Big Brother," a term for overreaching governmental authority. His thesis was predicated on political leaders expecting or demanding that "the people believe the absurd."

You don't know him as Eric Blair, but by his pen name George Orwell, a sharp political essayist with a *warning about the future of human freedom*. He asserted that we may not be strong enough, wise enough, or moral enough to cope with the kind of power we have learned to amass.

Consider orbiting satellites that can read the numbers on automobile license plates, computers which can tap into telephone and telefax transmissions, and many other exotic computer functions way beyond the average person's comprehension.

THE NEW WORLD ORDER

What does all of this mean? The loss of personal freedom and liberty, and the surrender of our national status and recognition.

Orwell's warnings were: BIG BROTHER IS WATCHING YOU! THE THOUGHT POLICE! WAR IS PEACE! Nearly every prediction of the 1949 essay has come to fruition in chilling reality.

Constantly we are hearing and reading about the New World Order, or global community. The repetitiveness of this buzz slogan is slowly sinking in. The world is heading to an international finance and political system, exactly as the Bible predicted nearly 2000 years ago.

> We stand today at a unique and extraordinary moment. The crisis in the Persian Gulf, as grave as it is, offers a rare opportunity to move toward an historic period of cooperation. Out of these troubled times a New World Order can emerge. A new era, free from threat of terror, stronger in the pursuit of justice. An era in which the nations of the world, east and west, north and south, can prosper and live in harmony.
>
> A hundred generations have searched for this elusive path to peace, while a thousand wars raged across the span of human endeavor. And today that New World Order is struggling to be born. A world where the rule of law supplants the rule of the jungle. A world in which nations recognize the shared responsibility for freedom and justice. A world where the strong respects the right of the weak... this crisis is the first assault on the New World that we seek.

These stunning words by President George Bush to the House and Senate in January 1991 coincide with Bible prophecy regarding end times.

CHARISMATIC SUPERLEADER

God's Word predicts that a super-charismatic leader-of-all-leaders will emerge from one of the nations of the world. His following will be unparalleled. The magnetism with which he captures the confidence of the international community will be unprecedented. Initially this man will seem to be an angel sent from God providing key answers to the dilemmas haunting mankind. As I see it, he will be an expert in finance and multinational people management, and will exude charm and brilliant sophistication. The Bible calls this dominant world leader the Antichrist.

The setting for Revelation chapter 13 takes place midway in the tribulation period. After the coming of Christ for His church (the rapture) there will be seven years when the judgments of God will be poured out on this earth.

It is only after the rapture that the Antichrist is revealed to this world. Second Thessalonians 2:3 states, "Let no one in any way deceive you, for it will not come unless the apostasy comes first, and the man of lawlessness is revealed, the son of destruction."

At the outset the Antichrist will confirm a covenant with the Jews for seven years. Daniel 9:27 reads, "He will make a firm covenant with the many for one week, but in the middle of the week he will put a stop to sacrifice and grain offering; and on the wing of abominations will come one who makes desolate, even until a complete destruction, one that is decreed, is poured out on the one who makes desolate." The term "week" in this setting is believed by many Bible scholars to mean "week of years" rather than "week of days." The Hebrew word translated for "week" means "seven." It is unrestricted, so it could mean seven days, weeks, or years. However, as in Genesis 29:27,28, where Jacob served one "week" of seven years for Rachel, Daniel 9:27's appearance of "week" almost certainly means "seven years."

The moment the covenant with the Jews is confirmed officially begins what the Bible calls the tribulation, or the seventieth week of Daniel (more about this later). This covenant is ostensibly to allow the Jews to live in peace in their homeland, unharmed by their surrounding enemies for seven years. But in the middle of that seven-year covenant the Antichrist breaks his pledge with the Jews. By this act of breaking the covenant, the last half of the tribulation begins, referred to by Jesus as the Great Tribulation.

It is clear that the setting for Revelation chapter 13 takes place when the covenant is broken at the beginning of the second 3½-year period.

Several notable characteristics regarding the Antichrist are evident from Revelation 13.

ANTICHRIST IS A MAN

According to this revealing chapter, the Antichrist is a man. In fact, in these 18 verses there are at least 11 masculine personal pronouns used to convey who the Beast is.

Verse 1 states, "*His* horns...*his* heads." Verse 2 states, "The beast which I saw...*his* feet...*his* mouth." Verse 3, "*his* heads...*his* fatal wound." Verse 6, "*He* opened *his* mouth." Verse 7, "It was given to *him* to make war with the saints and to overcome them; and authority over every tribe and people and tongue and nation was given to *him*." Verse 8, "All who dwell on the earth will worship *him*...." Verse 17, "The number of *his* name."

As in history gone by, there have been a number of lethal world leaders swaying the masses by their popular opinion. Yet Mussolini, Hitler, Stalin, Khadafy, and Saddam Hussein will all seem like Sunday school beginners next to this satanically energized superman.

ANTICHRIST'S NUMBER IS 666

The number 6 is the number of man, according to the Bible. Man was created on the sixth day, and everything man does comes up with the number 6, the number indicating failure. The number for God is 7, representing perfection, an excellent reflection of Deity. For example, on the seventh day God rested, and it was good.

There have been many scam formulas propagated throughout evangelical circles around the number 666. Just as Scripture plainly says that *no one* knows the day or the hour of the coming of the Lord, so I'm convinced that *no one* at present knows who the Antichrist is. Furthermore, biblical prophecy and integrity are often discredited by these sincere but misinformed enthusiasts.

As I have said, the Antichrist will *not* be revealed until he makes a seven-year covenant with the Jewish nation (Daniel 9:27). At that point the bride of Christ, the church, will be gone from the earth worldwide! So we may never actually know who the Antichrist is until sometime after that point.

Nevertheless, the number of the Antichrist is 666. Revelation 13:18 says, "Here is wisdom. Let him who has understanding calculate the number of the beast, for the number is that of a man; and his number is six hundred and sixty six."

Verses 16 and 17 state, "And he [the false prophet, the Antichrist's facilitator] causes all, the small and the great, and the rich and the poor, and the free men and the slaves, to be given a mark on their right hand, or on their forehead, and he provides that no one should be able to buy or sell except the one who has the mark, either the name of the beast or the number of his name."

So the number 666 during the tribulation will be a census number; every person will be cataloged into subordination and record. Right now in Brussels, Belgium, occupying three stories of the Common Market Building, is a computer which has the capacity to keep a written history of every living person on the globe.

The number 666 will be a finance number, perhaps invisibly tattooed on every person's right hand or forehead. The exclusivity of this 666 finance number means that under the Antichrist's mandate a person will not be able to buy or sell unless he or she has that number.

Innumerable articles in every major magazine and newspaper have predicted a cashless society for America and the world. With the extinction of currency, replaced by a finance number, crime would decrease. How can you rob a store operated by financial computerization?

> CURRENCY: It's not ready yet, but there is some planning being done on a world common currency. It's called Operation 666, and coincidentally, the World Bank code assigned to the project is also labeled "666." Preliminary reports say it's linked to credit cards and the cashless, paperless and proofless society. There is even a document in the wings called the Atlantic Union Treaty which mentions the common currency and, surprisingly enough, an International Court System.[1]

More recently, word regarding the popular and growing "Supersmart Card," developed 61 million units strong in Japan and Europe for Visa International, has been reported and tested in the U.S. The "Supersmart Card" allows you to pay for charges, perform foreign-currency conversions, operate the phone, and make airline reservations. The French and Japanese versions even store the computerized equivalent of "coins" to operate custom telephones, parking meters, and vending machines.

The optical card, another computer wizardry variety, encodes information (the equivalent of a thousand or more pages of double-spaced text) in a minute, rainbow-colored patterned readable by a laser beam.

> "By 1995," says Randy Boyett, vice president of Micro Card Technologies in Dallas, "half the people on the street may have a smart card in their pockets. The U.S. Department of Agriculture will soon launch a pilot program to issue food stamps as smart cards. Each recipient would receive a card programmed with a month's worth of benefit dollars, along with a personal identification number. The shopper would plug the card into a store's computer terminal, which would verify his identity and subtract the purchase from the card's memory chip."[2]

The convenient economic cashless system will play right into the Antichrist's hand. Today's rapidly developing technology confirms what was once deemed an impossibility. Remember, "without the mark they will not be able to buy or sell."

DESCRIPTION OF ANTICHRIST

Revelation 13:1 says, "I saw a beast coming up out of the sea...." In the Bible, the sea is a picture of the raging nations. Revelation 17:15 says, "The waters which you saw where the harlot sits are peoples and multitudes and nations and tongues." As the nations are in turmoil, the Antichrist will arise. And this Antichrist is known by many names.

The King of Babylon (Isaiah 14:4), the Little Horn (Daniel 7:8; 8:9), the Man of Sin, the Son of Perdition (2 Thessalonians 2:3 KJV), the Antichrist (1 John 2:18), and the Beast are just a few of the names for the evil one to come, according to Scripture.

The Antichrist is called a "beast" because that is what he is in the sight of God—a ruthless, unfeeling dictator. His true diabolical nature is exposed in wide-screen horror in the latter part of the tribulation period. He will pretend to be a great friend of Israel for the first $3\frac{1}{2}$ years of the tribulation, but deceptively he will turn on God's chosen people, the Jews. It is at this point that the Antichrist will be personally indwelt by Satan. Imagine the cunning deception as Lucifer stretched in skin launches his worldwide scheme of horror and domination!

The Antichrist will enter the newly rebuilt Jewish temple and place a statue of himself in the Holy of Holies and proclaim himself as god! From that point on he will demand that all people worship him and his image. And due to his miracles defying natural human laws, people will line up to bow in worship and profess spiritual obedience.

Revelation 13:3,4 says, "I saw one of his heads as if it had been slain, and his fatal wound was healed. And the whole earth was amazed and followed after the beast... saying, 'Who is like the beast, and who is able to wage war with him?'" The Antichrist's self-healing miracle will hypnotize the people into trancelike conformity and obedience.

In recent times we have seen brief expressions of charmers and their power over the general public. Jim Jones' cult charisma caused over 900 blinded followers to plunge to a suicidal death. Even the Jim Morrison delusion lingers, as does that of James Dean. But the Antichrist will exceed all others, totally deceiving the masses.

By demanding self-worship in the rebuilt temple the Antichrist will display the ultimate in blasphemy which could happen to the nation of Israel, as predicted by Daniel

9:27 and Jesus in Matthew 24:15. In Jewish terminology this is called "the abomination of desolation."

DURATION OF ANTICHRIST

Revelation 13:5 says, "There was given to him a mouth speaking arrogant words and blasphemies; and authority to act for forty-two months was given to him." Forty-two months is 3½ years! In the very middle of the tribulation the Antichrist's tranquil mask is removed. Suddenly he turns on the nation of Israel. To the approval of other nations the sacrificial system is stopped. Instead the Antichrist demands only to be worshiped.

It is this latter 3½-year period that is referred to in Scripture as *the Great Tribulation*. Jesus quoted this blasphemous act as "the abomination of desolation" (Matthew 24:15). In a tragic 42-month era the Antichrist will seek to totally exterminate Israel. Every calamity of the past pales compared to the horror of trouble during these final months before the return of Christ (Revelation 19:11).

The Antichrist will rule from Jerusalem, which historically has been God's holy city. Revelation 11:1,2 says, "There was given me a measuring rod like a staff; and someone said, 'Rise and measure the temple of God, and the altar, and those who worship in it. And leave out the court which is outside the temple, and do not measure it, for it has been given to the nations; and they will tread under foot the holy city for forty-two months.'"

The Jewish temple rebuilt before this will be made the capital building of the Antichrist. Daniel 8:11,12 says, "It even magnified itself to be equal with the Commander of the host; and it removed the regular sacrifice . . . and it will fling truth to the ground and perform its will and prosper."

The death, destruction, and devastation during this time will exceed that of all the previous wars of mankind. Researchers have calculated the death toll according to the prophecies in Revelation, and have concluded that one of every two people on earth will die. "And there will be a time of distress such as never occurred since there was a nation until that time" (Daniel 12:1).

Infusing the Antichrist with power will be Satan himself: "The dragon gave him his power and his throne and great authority" (Revelation 13:2). "And they worshiped the dragon, because he gave his authority to the beast; and they worshiped the beast, saying, 'Who is like the beast, and who is able to wage war with him?'" (Revelation 13:4).

Rebellion to or rejection of the Antichrist or his controlling mark will result in certain death. Verse 15 says, "There was given to him to give breath to the image of the beast, that the image of the beast might even speak and cause as many as do not worship the image of the beast to be killed." The reinstituted form of capital punishment will be the guillotine. What a visual, horrific deterrent to anyone attempting to defect from obedient submission to the Antichrist! I believe there will be televised executions of Antichrist-rejecters. Coupled with nightly miraculous reports of the Antichrist's unexplainable power and feats, the general public will rush forward in homage toward him.

This is exactly where the mark of the beast comes in. It is this unifying mark, easily readable, that will expose any rebels. What a perfect system! And the stage is already being set by advance planning and development of the cashless society.

DOMINION OF ANTICHRIST

Notice verse 3b, "The whole earth was amazed and

followed after the beast." Verse 7 reads, "And it was given to him to make war with the saints and to overcome them; and authority over *every* tribe and people and tongue and nation was given him." Verse 8 adds, "And all who dwell on the earth will worship him."

Recently I sat in the Minneapolis office of John Corts, the executive director of the Billy Graham Evangelistic Association. John glowingly informed me of Mr. Graham's far-reaching Hong Kong Crusade of 1990. In this *one* crusade Billy Graham preached the gospel via satellite transmission to the equivalent number of people that he had addressed in person during his entire previous ministry! Over 100,000 people converged on the Hong Kong stadium (seating only 25,000), but the audience receiving the message through satellite transmission numbered over 100,000,000 people!

Tragically, the Antichrist will harness the most sophisticated communication technology to wield his spellbinding effect on the world's population. His dominion will be worldwide. Imagine the impact of nightly visual reports of the Antichrist's miracles defying natural laws! Satan's Superman will speak "arrogant words," and the world will line up to accept him as the eternal man of the hour.

What will his dominion include? Principally three strategic areas reinforcing his diabolical control: a world government, a world church, and a world market.

Some suggest that the world government may restrict itself to the ten united European countries with a steamroller financial influence—what is more recently termed "the United States of Europe." Revelation 17:12,13 says, "The ten horns which you saw are ten kings, who have not yet received a kingdom, but they receive authority as kings with the beast for one hour. These have one purpose, and they give their power and authority to the beast."

The rapid formation of the new world order has a frightening correlation to this specific text. God's Word penned nearly 2000 years ago is as contemporary as the front page of the *London Times* or the *Wall Street Journal!*

The world government will execute the Antichrist's command. Energized by Satan, his governmental power will transcend all national boundaries of the past.

The world church will be a prostituted, impure spiritual harlot. Sound doctrine (Bible teaching) will be replaced by blasphemous teaching denying Christ and God. The only cardinal truth will be the supremacy of the Antichrist's person. His word will be verbatim scripture. What a stroke of captivation—the Antichrist will be a governmental, spiritual, and financial potentate! How could anyone reject his authority?

"And one of the seven angels who had the seven bowls came and spoke with me, saying, 'Come here, I shall show you the judgment of the great harlot who sits on many waters'" (Revelation 17:1). The old-time religion will be verbally scourged by the Antichrist. "And he [Antichrist] opened his mouth in blasphemies against God, to blaspheme His name and His tabernacle, that is, those who dwelt in heaven" (Revelation 13:6).

The Antichrist will exert his influence through a world market. The mark of the beast ensures that no one will be able to buy or sell without being branded. Verse 17 says, "He [Antichrist] provides that *no one* should be able to buy or sell except the one who has the mark, either the name of the beast or the number of his name." All of this speaks of total control. Slowly the Antichrist will amass such influence that he will attempt to fight even against Jesus Christ arrayed with an army of the redeemed at the second coming ending the tribulation: "I saw the beast and the kings of the earth and their armies, assembled to make war against Him who sat upon the horse, and against His army" (Revelation 19:19).

DESTRUCTION OF ANTICHRIST

Who could possibly overthrow someone so powerful with all of Satan's backing? The Lord Jesus Christ, God's eternal, obedient Son. The Bible comforts us with the fact that although all of these plagues and scary days are coming, the victory through Christ is certain! The Antichrist will reign, but only for a limited time. Man, as he always has, will have a volitional choice to say yes or no, to live eternally with Christ or die.

At the end of seven years the Antichrist will be destroyed. Sorrowfully, masses of deceived humanity will enter eternity separated from God because they succumbed to his evil deception. "And the beast was seized, and with him the false prophet who performed the signs in his presence, by which he deceived those who had received the mark of the beast and those who worshiped his image; these two were thrown alive into the lake of fire which burns with brimstone. And the rest were killed with the sword which came from the mouth of Him who sat upon the horse, and all the birds were filled with their flesh" (Revelation 19:20,21).

In February 1991 NBC aired a four-hour miniseries entitled "Love, Lies, and Murder." It was an icy-cold, disturbingly true story of a bizarre family murder plot. The story line was of a father, David Brown, and two teenage girls. Brown's story laid bare the dark side of the human psyche as it explored a complex cause of manipulation, mendacity, and homicide that unfolded in a Southern California family from 1985 to 1990.

The father, David Brown, manipulated sexually not only his young teenage daughter, and coached her to kill his wife, but actually persuaded his wife's own teenage sister to assist in the murder. The California judge who sentenced David Brown to life in prison without the possibility for parole said, "Mr. Brown, you are a scary person! That's the best way I can put it. Take Charley Manson—he looks crazy. You look saner than your defense attorney. I have seen it all, but I don't know. To get your own daughter to kill your wife, to get a young girl to assist in taking the life of her own sister—that makes Charley Manson look like a piker. There is no doubt in my mind that you, despite your normal, pleasant personality, are just a master manipulator."

Don't misinterpret the term "beast" for the Antichrist. No con man will be smoother or more cunning than the Antichrist. Energized by Satan himself, Mr. Charm is the true alias for the Beast, and his ultimate destruction is certain.

10

Those Poisonous Vials

◆ ━━━━━━━━━━━━━━━━━━━━━━━━ ◆

I heard a loud voice from the temple, saying to the seven angels, 'Go and pour out the seven bowls of the wrath of God into the earth.' And the first angel went and poured his bowl into the earth; and it became a loathsome and malignant sore upon the men who had the mark of the beast and who worship his image. And the second angel poured out his bowl into the sea, and it became blood like that of a dead man; and every living thing in the sea died. And the third angel poured out his bowl into the rivers and the springs of waters; and they became blood. And I heard the angel of the waters saying, 'Righteous art Thou, who art and who wast, O Holy One, because Thou didst judge these things; for they poured out the blood of saints and prophets, and Thou hast given them blood to drink. They deserve it.' And I heard the altar saying, 'Yes, O Lord God, the Almighty, true and righteous are Thy judgments.' And the fourth angel poured out his bowl upon the sun, and it was given to it to scorch men with fire. And men were scorched with fierce heat; and they blasphemed the name of God, who has the power over these plagues; and they did not repent, so as to give Him glory. And the fifth angel poured out his bowl upon the throne of the beast; and his kingdom became darkened; and they gnawed their tongues because of pain, and they blasphemed the God of heaven because of their pains and their sores; and they did not repent of their deeds. And the sixth angel poured out his bowl upon the great river, the Euphrates; and its water was dried up, that the way might be prepared for the kings from the east. And I saw coming out of the mouth of the dragon and out of the mouth of the beast and out of the mouth of the false prophet three unclean spirits like frogs; for they are spirits of demons, performing signs, which go out to the kings of the whole world, to gather them together for the war of the great day of God, the Almighty...."

"And the seventh angel poured out his bowl upon the air; and a loud voice came out of the temple from the throne, saying, 'It is done.' And there were flashes of lightning and sounds and peals of thunder; and there was a great earthquake, such as there had not been since man came to be upon the earth, so great an earthquake was it, and so mighty. And the great city was split into three parts, and the cities of the nations fell. And Babylon the great was remembered before God, to give her the cup of the wine of His fierce wrath. And every island fled away, and the mountains were not found. And huge hailstones, about one hundred pounds each, came down from heaven upon men; and men blasphemed God because of the plague of the hail, because its plague was extremely severe" (Revelation 16:1-14, 17-21).

The horror of the tribulation! Read every word carefully in the passage cited above. Man has had his day of fun, play, and rejecting God. The tribulation is God's time of vindicated wrath. We do not like the concept of the wrath of God, but it is clearly revealed in Scripture. God judges sin; His holy character has never changed.

So awful will this period of time be that Jesus said there has never been anything like it since the world began (Matthew 24:21). Daniel states that it will be a time of distress unequaled in history.

After the removal of Christians from this planet, God will begin His judgment plan upon the earth. Revelation chapter 6 coincides with the vials, bowls, or wrath found here in chapter 16. Remember, these are judgment vials designed for men and women who rejected God's Son and accepted the Antichrist.

VIAL 1: SORES

Verse 2 clearly states that the followers of the Antichrist will be stricken with grievous sores. What kind of sores are these? I concur with many others that there may be tactical nuclear activity during the tribulation period. Perhaps scaling, decomposing flesh falling from people's bodies due to radioactivity is seen here. Lesions and pus-filled sores dripping with infection will torment millions.

Unrepentant man will march on in sinful perversion right up to this point. AIDS and HIV will be pandemic. I personally feel that this verse refers to the 21 sexually transmitted diseases (STD's) ravaging several nations presently. With people racing down the trail of sensuality, the sores from STD's will intensify. Amsterdam now wants to make its window shopping prostitution trade into a recognized business!

Perhaps the use of chemical weapons during the tribulation is also in view here. Saddam Hussein has used them on some of his own people in Iraq. The photos I've viewed have an eerie similarity to this verse. Will the Antichrist push the button of chemical detonation, leaving multitudes dead?

VIAL 2: DEATH OF THE OCEANS

Verse 3 is mind-boggling! As the angel pours his vial into the world's seas, everything dies and becomes like the blood of dead men—a dark, nauseous appearance.

What smell is there that can compare with dead fish! But we're not talking about a dozen or so here; we're talking about every living thing in the sea dying! Imagine ... the smell, the decomposing sea life viewed everywhere. This will cause a marine holocaust. Think for a moment of the disease and bacteria promoted because of this judgment. As the wind sweeps across the Pacific and Atlantic oceans the aroma of death will fill the nostrils of people on earth's various continents.

VIAL 3:
POISONING OF ALL FRESH WATER

Verses 4 through 7 bring down the hammer blow of contaminated fresh water throughout the world. *No more drinking water!* Of course many people will try to imbibe in spite of the poisoning, and they will die.

VIAL 4: BLISTERING HEAT

Verses 8 and 9 describe a heat wave that undoubtedly will leave many people dead. This summer in Kansas we hit a record 105 degrees, and we had deaths. But in this time of judgment the sun will scorch people. Perhaps the temperature will climb to 125 or 150.

Here again, I see a connection to nuclear activity. There is little doubt that tactical nuclear weapons will be utilized in the tribulation. The result? A heat furnace unlike anything man has ever known.

VIAL 5:
ANTICHRIST'S CAPITAL DARKENED

Verses 10 and 11 tell of God darkening the capital of the Antichrist. This, of course, is Jerusalem. In other words, the sun will not shine at all upon the Antichrist's world headquarters. Some see this blackout spreading throughout the entire revived Roman empire—all of Europe, the "ten toes" who aligned with the Antichrist. Perhaps this will pave the way for the war of all wars, Armageddon. Maybe the 200 million soldiers from the east, possibly Japan joined with China, will secretly move into battle position as the blackout continues.

VIAL 6:
EUPHRATES RIVER DRIED UP

Verses 12 through 16 describe several things. First, the great Euphrates River, something of a geographical roadblock, will be dried up, becoming the bridge of opportunity for the kings of the East to march against the Antichrist. God facilitates this by drying the entire river!

Furthermore, at this point demonic spirits come out of the mouth of the Antichrist, performing astounding miracles. These demonically disguised spectacles rally the kings of the West and other parts of the world to back the Antichrist for the war of all wars.

VIAL 7:
WORLD'S GREATEST EARTHQUAKE

Verses 17 through 21 describe a natural tragedy that will affect the land, the seas, the atmosphere, and the punished people on the earth: The greatest earthquake of all time will hit the earth. Entire islands will disappear and numerous cities will fall. The death toll from this vial will no doubt be in the millions. Hailstones 100 pounds in weight will crush buildings, vehicles, and people.

Fear and paranoia will shoot through every person. "A day of wrath is that day, a day of trouble and distress, a day of destruction and desolation, a day of darkness and gloom, a day of clouds and thick darkness" (Zephaniah 1:15).

These judgments remind us that we must thank the Lord every day that He has redeemed us, for judgment pervades the entire book of Revelation. In spite of these torturous judgments, we read that men repented not. Instead, they screamed obscenities and blasphemies in the face of God.

The Bible tells us that it is the goodness of God that leads us to repentance. How good God has been to open our eyes! We are going to miss this terror! Let's persuade every person we can to come to Christ *now* while there is still time. We can't be negligent. Let's *go tell*!

11

The Occultic Bonanza

✦ ══════════════════════ ✦

Standing over Joey's damaged body in a hospital in a Southern state, I had to fight nausea. His 18-year-old comatose body was pathetically pale, and accumulated days in a nonresponsive state had his limbs curling unnaturally. Like nearly half a million other American teenagers per year, Joey had attempted to kill himself.

Joey's method was to hang himself—rarely chosen by kids wanting to exit the headaches of modern life. It was a Saturday night. Mom was in the kitchen frying hamburgers. The whole family was to gather at 8:00 P.M. for a late dinner. Joey took his jam box in the family bathroom with him. "Fade to Black," Metallica's suicide-laced song, was pulsating through the shower wall. No big deal—Joey always listened to his music while he showered. His room was littered with posters of many groups like that of his selection that day.

The school photo his mom showed me of a more healthy Joey had him in a heavy-metal T-shirt. Cascading past his shoulders was his jet-black hair, and he wore a wry smile on his face.

"I heard a banging on the wall, Jerry," his exhausted

mother told me as she stood across the bedside from me. Even while we talked we seldom looked at each other. Joey's semicomatose body commanded all our attention. I noticed that the tracheotomy was misting with the oxygen forced into his system. Occasionally he would turn to me and snarl; perhaps it was an incoherent response.

Joey's mom had interpreted the knocking on the wall during the running of the shower water to mean "Turn off the hot water." (One of the idiosyncracies of their home was that if you turned on the hot water in one area of the house it would go cold in another.)

Obligingly, she reached up and squeezed the kitchen faucet off. Several minutes later, impulsively, sensing that something was wrong, she raced to the door of the family bathroom. "JOEY!" she screamed. "JOEY! JOEY!" There was no reply—only the dancing water gurgling in the drain competing with the audacious music.

The tone of her voice, more than the volume, caused the entire family to rendezvous at the door. In desperation they kicked the locked door open. Joey was jerking in the final moments of nearly 12 minutes of strangulation. Next to his jam box was this letter he wrote to Ozzy Osborne, the prince of heavy-metal music:

Dear Ozzy: (your name's even tattooed on my arm)

Keep Rocking. Please write back, man. I'm counting on your answer, bud. Just a brief letter to let you know you are a rock legend and you are my biggest influence in life. I think so much of you. I have every record and love every song. I'm not blaming you, but I even started worshiping Satan, cause if you go to hell I want to burn with you. If you could would you write me a letter on who you worship; so I can worship him, too. . . . it's not because of you, but I'm sick of life so I'm going to commit suicide, and I want to know before I do where you are going, so I can, too. If you still worship Satan then I will keep him as my leader and burn. Love your music. You're the best, dude.

Love, True Ozzy fan,

Joey

Representing a whole new cadre of the American young, Joey had "turned on" to the devil much like kids turn on to drugs. We are now witnessing an international phenomenon: Satan worship is in vogue.

THE EMERGING DARK SCENARIO

Whereas once it was just preachers exclaiming the rise of demonic interest, now professionals from many different human interest fields attest to a bizarre emerging dark scenario. Mental health workers have counseled thousands of generational satanic victims. Like the scarlet thread of incest passed multigenerationally in many families, so it is with satanic worship.

A 1989 *Seventeen* magazine survey found that 12 percent of teenagers have "some or a lot of faith" in Satanism. America looked on as ABC's "20/20" played a videotaped exorcism performed by a veteran Catholic exorcist in April 1991. Such movies, birthed by the 1973 thriller *The Exorcist*, have hit the theaters like a tidal wave.

> Overall, levels of belief in demons are quite high among Americans: 55 percent believe that the devil exists, 37 percent do not and 7 percent are not sure. Figures do not add to 100 because some people did not answer.

Almost as many Americans—49 percent—believe it is possible for people to be possessed by the devil, while 35 percent do not believe in possession and 15 percent are not sure.

Ten percent of Americans believe that they have talked with the devil or that the devil has talked to them, and 89 percent do not believe this has happened to them.[1]

Scores of teenagers across North America have committed suicide in Satan's name. Numerous young Luciferians have murdered parents or friends in their allegiance to the devil. When I videotaped with Sean Sellers on death row in the Oklahoma State Penitentiary, he told me he killed his parents because he loved them. Just a spry 17 at the time, Sean gunned down his mom and dad in the wee hours of the morning with a .38 pistol.

THE EDGE OF EVIL

Scripture teaches that Satan worship will be widespread during the tribulation era: "They worshiped the dragon [a name for Satan], because he gave authority to the beast" (Revelation 13:4). Furthermore, the whole world will worship the Beast (Satan's man, the Antichrist) during this time: "All who dwell on the earth will worship him, everyone whose name has not been written from the foundation of the world in the book of life of the Lamb who has been slain" (Revelation 13:8).

When I spotted teenage satanic dabblers in my public school assembly talks throughout the nation, I felt that something definitive needed to be written on Satanism. I took nearly a year to write *The Edge of Evil: The Rise of Satanism in North America*. That book, now in many subsequent printings, has been used by criminologists, mental health therapists, doctors, and clergymen. *The Edge of Evil* was a compilation of nearly 100 interviews with Satanists themselves, multiple-personality specialists, and victims of occult activity.

Paul said in 1 Timothy 4:1, "The Spirit explicitly says that in later times some will fall away from the faith, paying attention to deceitful spirits and doctrines of demons." There are 227 references in the New Testament alone on the topic of the devil and demons.

Much of popular North American Satanism is to be credited to a former police photographer named Anton LaVey. Mr. LaVey officially founded the Satanic church in 1966 on California Street in San Francisco. Sammy Davis Jr. and Jayne Mansfield were two celebrities who were followers of Satanism at one time. Initially perceived as a religious genetic freak, the Satanic church now recruits and claims thousands of people coast-to-coast. LaVey's cardinal book, *The Satanic Bible*, has sold nearly a million paperback copies alone (Avon Books). LaVey has served as a consultant on several Hollywood films based on the occult world.

Religious Satanists like LaVey distance themselves publicly from any form of illegal activity. When I debated Zeena LaVey (Anton LaVey's daughter and a spokesperson for the Church of Satan) on KABC's AM Los Angeles in Southern California, she attempted to describe her church as a healthy opportunity for the young.

I reminded Zeena and the viewing audience that my own investigation, coupled with that of many others, found *The Satanic Bible* as the central book in virtually every teenage satanic homicide or suicide case. *The Satanic Bible* poses white or black magic as two venues for every aspiring Satanist. LaVey says, "White magic is supposedly utilized only for good or unselfish purposes, and black magic, we are told, is used only for selfish or 'evil' reasons." However, for the satanist there is no such dividing line. Magick is magick, be it used to help or hinder.

"During white magical ceremonies, the practitioners stand within a pentagram to protect themselves from the evil forces which they call for help. To the satanist, it seems a bit two-faced to call on these forces to help while at the same time protecting yourself from the very powers you have asked for assistance. The satanist realizes that *only* by putting himself in league with these forces can he fully and unhypocritically utilize the Powers of Darkness to his best advantage" (*The Satanic Bible*).

Imagine a teenager reading the *Satanic Bible* and the impression it leaves! It is hair-raising to read LaVey's words on page 88 of the *Satanic Bible*: "The only time a satanist would perform a human sacrifice would be if it were to serve a two-fold purpose, that being to release the magician's wrath in the throwing of a curse and, more important, to dispose of a totally obnoxious and deserving individual."

ACCEPTING THE SATANIC CHALLENGE

Several young people have accepted the satanic challenge. Richard Rameriz, the drifter from El Paso known as the infamous Night Stalker, was convicted of killing more than ten people in Satan's name. Jim Hardy, Pete Roland, and Ron Clements of Carl Junction, Missouri, sacrificed Steven Newberry and dumped him in their "well of hell" on the edge of town. In Jefferson Township, New Jersey, 14-year-old Tommy Sullivan slit his wrists after he butchered his mother in the basement with his Boy Scout knife. His note said he had seen a vision of Satan and was ordered to preach it to his friends. Theresa Simmons of Douglas

County, Georgia, now spending life in prison, participated in the coven ceremony of killing another teen.

And these are just a few of the stories. I have lectured on the occult in 117 cities throughout the country. The most horrible story I encountered was in Eugene, Oregon. The former religion professor of the University of Oregon, a Princeton graduate, is now behind bars. Convicted of sexual abuse linked to occultic activity, I met the victim—his daughter—nine, with beautiful blonde hair. She stood in front of me in Eugene with her mother, sobbing, "He made me kill babies."

The following is only what has been reported. Only God knows how much activity is going on behind closed doors. Dr. Larry Pazder, a Victoria, British Columbia, psychiatrist who coined the term "ritual abuse" for the psychiatric community a decade ago, says that over the years he has treated 300 to 400 patients who claim they were ritually abused.

A leading North American expert on the diagnosis and treatment of ritual abuse, Pazder has consulted in more than a thousand cases, mostly from the United States.

Regarding the issue of human sacrifice, no one can quantitatively reveal the number of satanic homicides annually. Dr. Willi Gutowski, a Chilliwack General Hospital psychiatrist (Chilliwack, B.C.), says that evidence-gathering is nearly impossible because cults go to extreme lengths to cover up the remains of people that are murdered, especially babies. According to Gutowski, at conferences psychiatrists are hearing survivors pointing to the fact that prominent people are involved in cult activities. These include mayors, lawyers, police, church people, and other upstanding citizens.

Anton LaVey, as well as many other Satanists worldwide, received much of their inspiration from a bisexual fanatic in the United Kingdom by the name of Aliester Crowley (born October 12, 1875, died December 1, 1947). Crowley's parents were Plymouth Brethren Christians who nicknamed their uncontrollable son "the Beast." Crowley shocked England by practicing his own brand of devil worship, and left behind several volumes. Crowley said, "For the highest spiritual working one must accordingly choose that victim which contains the greatest and purest force. A male child perfect in innocence and of high intelligence is the most satisfactory and suitable victim. It is a mistake to suppose that the victim is injured. On the contrary, this is the most blessed and merciful of all deaths, for the elemental spirit is directly built up in the Godhead."

Crowley also espoused, "Do what thou wilt. Good is evil and evil is good. Thou hast no right but to do thy will. Do that and no other shall say nay. Man has the right to live by his own will, eat what he will, think what he will, love as he will. Man has the right to kill those who would thwart these rights."

SATAN ON THE OFFENSE

According to the Bible, as this age draws to a close, Satan will work in an extremely aggressive way to blind men's minds from the truth. It is easy to see a satanic agenda in much of the music and entertainment upon which young people feed today. When *Time* magazine wrote about how violent youth are today, they pointed out source areas:

> *Movies and TV*—many boys have their first sexual experience while watching sadistic slasher films at gross-out parties. By age 16, a child has seen 200,000 acts of violence on television.

Recorded music—Guns N' Roses' "It's So Easy" orders, "Turn around bitch I got a use for you/Besides you ain't got nothin' better to do/And I's bored." 2 Live Crew in "We Want Some Pussy" sings, "The girls would say 'Stop' I'd say, 'I'm not.'"

Comic books—women in scenes of bondage and torture are standard fare today.

Society has generally been able to control and channel aggressive impulses through its basic institutions—home, schools, and church. But these moral pillars are crumbling. Today's children, unlike those of earlier generations, are fed a steady diet of glorified violence. Rock music has become a dominant—and potentially destructive—part of teenage culture. Lyrics, album covers and music videos, particularly in rock groups called heavy metal, romanticize bondage, sexual assaults and murder....

Among the most offensive purveyors of brutality to women are slasher films. The movies that inaugurated the trend, including Friday the 13th, Halloween and Nightmare on Elm Street, are now tame compared with such opuses as I Spit on Your Grave or Splatter University. The main features: graphic and erotic scenes of female mutilation, rape or murder. Slasher films are widely shown on cable TV, and video shops do a booming business in rentals, especially among 11 to 15 year-olds.[2]

Satan has mobilized an army of demons in the spirit realm (read Ephesians 6:10-12). His demons do everything imaginable to cloud the truth of Jesus Christ's love for people and His desire to cleanse and forgive them. I believe that Satan has a bull's-eye target on youth: The young generation is barraged with every type of message of gratification and filth, and the young generation is groping in spiritual darkness.

According to the National Center for Health Statistics, every 78 seconds a teenager attempts suicide, and every 90 seconds one succeeds. Every 80 minutes a teenager is murdered. Every 20 minutes a teenager becomes pregnant (45 percent get an abortion). And every two minutes a teenager will give birth.

WHAT THE BIBLE SAYS ABOUT SATAN

The Bible has a great deal to say about Satan. Originally Satan was an obedient angel of God, the leader of the angelic world. Isaiah 14:12-15 records how he led an insurrection against God brought on by pride. Ezekiel 28:12-18 is the most detailed biography of Lucifer in the entire Bible. This text, along with the progressive revelation of God, notes the following facts about Satan.

1. Lucifer was a created being. He was created perfect and designated as an anointed cherub. A cherub in Scripture denotes an angel that has an unusually close relationship to God (Ezekiel 28:14,15).

2. Lucifer was the wisest of the angelic hosts, and next to the Godhead the most powerful force in the universe (Ezekiel 28:12).

3. Lucifer was the most beautiful angel in appearance (Ezekiel 28:13). (Every stone resembles a different color; Lucifer was like a mobile rainbow.)

4. Lucifer sinned because of his beauty and pride (Ezekiel 28:17; see also Revelation 12:7-9).

The principal New Testament name for Lucifer is Satan, meaning "adversary." He is also revealed by many other names:

1. Roaring lion—1 Peter 5:8

2. Accuser—Revelation 12:10

3. Liar and murderer—John 8:44

4. God of this world—2 Corinthians 4:4

5. Enemy—Matthew 13:39

6. Angel of light or imitator—2 Corinthians 11:13-15

7. Tempter—Matthew 4:3

8. Angel of the abyss—Revelation 9:11

Assisting Satan are demons. Demons have:

1. Personalities—Mark 1:23,24

2. Intelligence—Matthew 12:44,45

3. Speaking ability—Acts 19:15

4. Ability to afflict physically—2 Corinthians 12:7

5. Ability to cause depression and suicide—Mark chapter 5

6. Emotion and fear—James 2:19

DEMONIC INVASION TACTICS

There are three invasion tactics that demons use on human beings. It is important to know them. My fear for some young people involved in the occult is that they unknowingly open themselves up to demon possession. Demons can:

1. Possess—Mark 5:1-13 ("legion" signified 3000 to 6000 individuals)

2. Oppress—Acts 10:38

3. Obsess—harass to sin

What happened to David Wiseman, 15, of Bessemer City, North Carolina? Stephen Huss commented that he noticed something different about his friend—he was distant, moody, distracted. He was really into his music, some of which contained Satanic references. The black-haired tenth-grader lit himself like a torch after pouring gasoline over his body.

Billy and Gail Staples, David's parents, found a one-page, handwritten note in his bedroom. David penned that he wasn't committing suicide, but was going to "live with the devil."

In Lethbridge, Alberta, Chilton Thur, 15, was found hanging in his girlfriend's basement on December 15, 1989. Chilton's lacerated arm spilled blood, and the words "TO LIVE IS TO DIE" were scrawled across his body in blood. Rhea Thur, the boy's mom, said her son had become obsessed with Satanist rituals.

"After that death, Wayne Townsend's body was found hanging in a group home on March 2. On March 8, 1990, less than 24 hours after Wayne's funeral, the body of Ashley Merrick was found hanging in his grandmother's basement."[3]

Was it possession? We don't know. In some instances Satan works in an overt and ghastly way. However, the Satanists I fear the most are *covert*. The more a Satanist gets absorbed in illegal behavior, the more normalized he seems on the outside. Demonstrative teenage dabblers are not the most lethal expression of the present-day occult movement.

Satan also works subtly. After all, he presents himself as an angel of light. The popular TV show "Twin Peaks," is alleged to have a deeper meaning. Writer Peter Howell, after watching every episode of Twin Peaks, claims he can answer the question of who killed Laura Palmer. But first, he claims, you have to know the basics:

> There is a coven of owl witches in the town of Twin Peaks, led by Satan himself. The clues to their existence are to be found in *A Dictionary of Symbols*, by J. E. Cirlot. (It is the Bible of symbols, numerology, and religious icons.) [Use] this ... [and] other useful leads, such as *Laura Palmer's Secret Diary*, and the Twin Peaks mysteries unfold.
>
> The witches that are causing all the mayhem worship owls, which are symbols of darkness. Coven members identify each other and their victims through the symbol of a broken circle, which represents Satan. Laura Palmer was their prey ("Children are prey sometimes," the Log Lady warned).
>
> The Owl cultists like to dress up in owl costumes ("Owls are sometimes big," the Log Lady said), and engage in sex orgies, drug deals, and satanic rituals in the woods around Twin Peaks, near a tree that symbolizes the gates of Hell. As Laura writes in her diary, she first encounters them when wife beater Leo Johnson blindfolds her and ties her to a chair in the woods, and everyone engages in an all-night orgy.
>
> There are 13 Owl Coven members. They include many well-known Twin Peaks residents ...

The Owls are led, of course, by Satan himself. He has taken up residence in Twin Peaks, which has a name referring to the twin horns on his forehead....[4]

Mr. Howell's suggestions may or may not be correct, but they are interesting food for thought.

ACTIVE BUT DOOMED

As we move toward the coming of Jesus Christ, Satan will be active. The seven years of tribulation will be his heyday. Nevertheless, Satan's day is coming. He is destined for destruction by God Himself.

At the end of the tribulation, John says, "I saw an angel coming down from heaven, having the key of the abyss and a great chain in his hand. And he laid hold of the dragon, the serpent of old, who is the devil and Satan, and bound him for a thousand years, and threw him into the abyss, and shut it and sealed it over him, so that he should not deceive the nations any longer, until the thousand years were completed; after these things he must be released for a short time" (Revelation 20:1-3). After he successfully tempts those who have enjoyed a thousand-year Utopian reign of Christ, Satan will finally be destroyed for eternity. Listen triumphantly to Revelation 20:10: "And the devil who deceived them was thrown into the lake of fire and brimstone, where the beast and the false prophets are also; and they will be tormented day and night forever and ever."

Thank God for the ultimate triumph of right over wrong!

12

Deceptive Preconditioning

✦ ━━━━━━━━━━━━━━━━━━━━━━━━━━ ✦

The Spirit explicitly says that in later times some will fall away from the faith, paying attention to deceitful spirits and doctrines of demons.

—1 Timothy 4:1

False prophets also arose among the people, just as there will also be false teachers among you, who will secretly introduce destructive heresies, even denying the Master who bought them, bringing swift destruction upon themselves. And many will follow their sensuality, and because of them the way of truth will be maligned; and in their greed they will exploit you with false words; their judgment from long ago is not idle, and their destruction is not asleep" (2 Peter 2:1-3).

Shirley MacLaine braces herself for another bestseller. Her seventh book, *Coming to Terms*, is sure to zing readers worldwide, as did her previous literary voyages on reincarnation and out-of-body experiences.

At 56 she is perhaps the best-known proponent of a speeding phenomenon known as the New Age movement.

Her claims are extraordinary: tales of previous life existences, of channeling's connective-power, and of asserting the spiritual dimension in one's life.

The 1980's experienced an explosion of New Age spiritualism. Regretfully, few Christians understand the danger and misleading trails in this sector of spiritual mysticism. Many consider New Age philosophy simply another dimension in Christianity, as if it were merely another denomination with some peculiar doctrinal distinctives.

But this is not the case at all. Satan is a cunning master imitator. Scripture teaches clearly that as we approach the end of the age there will be a great rise in "doctrines of demons." Unquestionably, the New Age movement fits this category as it uses many Christian terms in its propaganda.

THE NEW AGE IMPACT

Consider the incredible impact which the New Age movement is making on our society:

Annually Americans spend more money on books than on movies, and one hot commodity in literary circles is the New Age Publishing and Retail Alliance. This alliance, claiming over 50 different publishing houses, is flooding the market with hundreds of books advocating every angle of the New Age movement.

When I surveyed various New Age booths at the 1990 American Booksellers Convention in Las Vegas, I was stunned at their rapid growth in the marketplace. Over a billion dollars per year is being raked in by these books!

Forbes magazine estimates that the New Age market receives more than 3.4 billion dollars in sales each year. This amount would exceed *all* of the revenue represented by the *entire* Christian Booksellers Association, which represents the vast majority of evangelical publishers in our country today!

There are many buzzwords in New Age thought: do-it-yourself spirituality, coming in tune with one's self, channeling, mysticism, reincarnation, fire-walking, and meditation. Slowly the general public is being "evangelized" with this new gospel of self-help and spirituality.

There is advice for families, child-rearing, and interactive social relationships. The *St. Paul Pioneer Dispatch's* article "Child-Rearing in a New Age" voices editor Anne Caron's overview presented in her book *Spiritual Parenting in the New Age.*

> Spiritually attuned parents find even tarot cards [and] crystals offer no guarantees. New Age parents raise their children on the four winds, tarot cards, goddesses, and shimmering crystals. The spirit within they can't do without—but how to convey that nebulous concept to the kids?
>
> They wring their hands in worry: "What if little Johnny rebels and grows up to be, say, a devout Baptist or Catholic?" To the rescue comes "Spiritual Parenting in the New Age"...a guide for parents on the cutting edge—some might say fringe—of a broad New Age movement.
>
> New Age parents have special concerns: For instance, what do pagan moms and dads tell the relatives? "Use the language of diplomacy," Caron advises. "Say prayer, not magic or spell...say ceremony, not ritual. This way, I can tell my aunt that we had a blessing ceremony for our infant daughter under the auspices of a Dutch Reformed minister, leaving out the invocation to the

four elements, the sprinkling of cornmeal and the bestowal of a spirit name…"

New Age kids deserve New Age toys. Here's the latest in what should exist (and maybe has and always will on some far-flung astral plane), according to Laura Eisen and Mark Frey, smart-aleck authors of *Shopping for Enlightenment* (Celestial Arts).

Crystal pacifiers. For crying out loud! Everybody loves a baby. These astonishing crystals bring inner peace to your child and serenity to your surroundings.

Cosmic Barbie dolls. Every little girl's dream doll enters the New Age! New wardrobe items include Past Lives Barbie with period clothing selections and Trance-Medium Barbie with reversible head.

Self-love dolls. Doll fashioned in your own image (send a photo). Gives you unlimited opportunity to kiss, hug, and cuddle yourself. Has zippered pocket, which opens to reveal the god-within-you.

When they get older, how about Aura Cleansing Gel (to brighten and revitalize the aura); the Near-Death Simulator (enjoy all the benefits of a near-death experience in the comfort of your own home); the Inner-Voice Amplifer, the White Light Converter (harness your body's excess energy to run small household appliances).[1]

But the New Age movement stretches much further than toys for kids. The self-help success-seminar business is hotter now than it has ever been. Hotels are rented in every major city in the country to offer businessmen and women a greater edge. Enter New Age mind control techniques, the latest fad for corporate America. More than half of the 500 largest U.S. companies have adopted some form of New Age creativity training!

Some researchers suggest that up to 50 million Americans are New Age enthusiasts or sympathizers. This figure may be too high, but the number is certainly in the millions.

POWER IS THE KEY

As with Satanism, the word "power" is the key to understanding the New Age movement: *power* to transcend time and space; *power* to defy moral and physical laws; *power* to do anything with one's mind; even *power* to become a god! Firewalking is based on the premise that mental-spiritual power can transcend the heat of red-hot coals which the enthusiast treads. (Incidentally, firewalking is one of the most spiritual experiences which a mature New Ager can enjoy.)

Inseparably connected with *power* for the New Ager is the concept of *meditation* or *mind-control*. This is where the deluge of books on holistic healing and visualization come in. Holistic healing is based on the premise that all beings consist of cognitive physiological, emotional, and spiritual qualities. If these separate elements are mentally concentrated into one power through New Age meditation, healing will result.

Amazing cancer-cure stories are told by New Age authors, doctors, and patients. It is thought that the immune system can fight off bad cancer cells or any other debilitating disease through the power of meditation and the use of healing crystals.

In the book *The Relaxation Response,* noted Harvard Medical School professor Herbert Benson illustrates the contemporary New Age meditative process connected to the ancient art of Tibetan Buddhist monks. In unusually deep states of "heat yoga" (meditation) the zealous monks raised the temperature of their fingers and toes as much as 15 degrees without changing their bodies' core temperatures.

Some New Agers suggest that powerful arts of meditation can allow a person to enter the body of another individual. This was cinematically presented in the box-office smash *Ghost*.

Simply put, the New Age movement is a spiritual, political, and social revolution which clusters numerous occult/metaphysical groups together with the goal of transforming individuals through mystical enlightenment, thereby resulting in a new age of peace, harmony, and prosperity on earth.

One *USA Today* poll revealed that 14 percent of Americans believe in trance mediums. New Age trance channelers enter altered or semiconscious states to share a vision or special message of potential healing, happiness, or enlightenment. Ouija boards, crystal balls, automatic handwriting, and other occult paraphernalia are reportedly used by trance channelers. *Possession* is the goal of trance channeling, in which a personality other than the individual's is manifested when the goal has been achieved in this spiritism.

Crystals and crystal balls are thought to be conduits of cosmic energy with the ability to cure illnesses. New Agers contend that the body consists of crystallized thought patterns stored in the bones. Vibrations from crystals can replace negative patterns or energy.

So what is wrong and what is right with the New Age movement? As with most heretical movements, not every point of New Agers is bad, but the basic teaching of the New Age movement is foreign to God's Word. Furthermore, this pursued activity is a grand opportunity to enter the spirit world and be entertained by disguised demonic spirits.

Now let's look at some of the partial truths of the New Age movement.

PRESERVATION OF THE PLANET

David said in Psalm 24:1, "The earth is the Lord's, and all it contains, the world and those who dwell in it." Fundamental to our faith, philosophy, and worldview as Christians is the first verse in the Bible, "In the beginning God created the heavens and the earth" (Genesis 1:1).

Christians more than anyone should respect, protect, and keep clean the earth. It was created by the Lord; it did not evolve. In a sense we are watchkeepers over this beautiful planet. Additionally, this planet is the natural revelation of God. This planet is *not* God; but it does reveal the *existence* of God: "The heavens are telling of the glory of God, and their expanse is declaring the work of His hands" (Psalm 19:1).

LIVING IN PEACE

God commands us to live in peace with our fellowman: "Esteem them very highly in love because of their work. Live in peace with one another" (1 Thessalonians 5:13). War and conflict with other nations should be avoided if at all possible.

As Christians we realize that this world will never come to perfect peace until Christ returns (Revelation 19:11). The earth is not slowly maturing into a Utopia. Instead, sin is causing man to become worse. Only a behavioral change, by the new birth experience (John 3:3), can create godly living in any person's life.

As long as there is sin, there will be conflict and dishar-mony. Husseins, Hitlers, and other evil men will exist until Jesus Christ removes sin and evil from this world forever at His second coming.

ETHICS AND COMPASSION

Benevolence, ethics, and compassion are far more im-portant than monetary incentives. Homelessness should be the responsibility of the church first, not the government. It is a shame that any individual sleeps in the street with as many churches as there are in every city.

However, by doing good works we will not ensure a place in heaven or the afterlife for anyone: "For by grace you have been saved through faith; and that not of yourselves, it is the gift of God; not as a result of works, that no one should boast" (Ephesians 2:8,9).

We are *not* going to heaven by anything good or mer-itorious that we have done. We are going to heaven because Christ took our place at the cross, and bore our sins on Himself (1 Peter 3:18; 2 Corinthians 5:21).

EMPHASIS ON SPIRITUALITY

For far too long our society has acted as if man were simply a highly complex animal—an animal with no spiri-tual dimension or future eternal pilgrimage.

The New Age movement has pronounced the need for a renewed interest in the spiritual realm. No one more than a Christian could agree that there is a very real spiritual scenario behind the physical events of day-to-day life. The Bible reveals that there are angels—in fact several different kinds. Every believer in Jesus Christ has a guardian angel

(Hebrews 1:14). Some of us, by the way we drive our car, keep our angel on the edge! Scripture also reveals the reality of demon spirits which work against Christians and blind the unredeemed to their need of Christ.

In some instances, when one's spiritual life is in harmony with God, physical healing can occur through the power of prayer, but not through self-contrived meditation. Spiritual problems solved through Jesus Christ can cause alcohol, sex, or gambling addictions to cease.

According to Romans chapter 6, the law of sin is still at work in this world. Regardless if your resting pulse is 40 or 60, sooner or later you will die. Death is a reminder of the fact that "the wages of sin is death" (Romans 6:23).

A true Christian *cannot* embrace New Age teaching for many reasons. According to the Bible, the New Age movement is wrong in the following areas.

THE PERSON OF GOD

The Scriptures present God as a divine, almighty being who rules in the affairs of man: "In the beginning God..." (Genesis 1:1). God has always existed. Our finite minds cannot comprehend God. God is one eternal Being revealed in three Persons: God the Father, God the Son, God the Holy Spirit. This triunity of God is revealed in His creation of man: "Let Us make man in Our image [Father, Son, and Holy Spirit], according to Our likeness; and let them rule over the fish of the sea and over the birds of the sky and over the cattle and over all the earth" (Genesis 1:26).

God is *not* man's higher self. God is *not* an inner manifestation of divinity within man. God is not the world, nor is He impersonal or amoral. Man *cannot* become a god. Man, by the indwelling Holy Spirit, can become godly, but *never* God.

THE PERSON OF JESUS CHRIST

Jesus Christ is not an office, status of enlightenment, or avatar (manifestation of a god-guru). When we speak of Jesus Christ, we are referring to God's Son, eternally existent, who died on the cross, physically rose from the dead, and now sits at the right hand of the Majesty on High.

> By common confession great is the mystery of godliness: He [Jesus Christ] who was revealed in the flesh was vindicated in the Spirit, beheld by angels, proclaimed among the nations, believed on in the world, taken up in glory (1 Timothy 3:16).

Jesus Christ is the only Lord, the true God-man, the only Savior for man.

THE BIBLICAL VIEW OF MAN

Consistent with the Bible's teaching of God and His Son, Jesus Christ, man is *not* God in embryo. Man has been created by God from the dust of the earth, and to dust his physical body shall return: "God created man in His own image, in the image of God He created him; male and female He created them" (Genesis 1:27).

According to the Bible, man has fallen from God by sin and therefore must be redeemed, cleansed, and forgiven in order to enjoy fellowship with God. Without this redemption man will be lost eternally. Man is *not* all things, nor does man have the truth within himself. Man is not a sleeping god that needs to be aroused. Man is a sinner greatly loved by a caring, compassionate God who desires that no one should perish (1 John 3:16; Romans 5:8; John 3:16).

BIBLICAL CREATION

The physical realm we see is *not* a part of God; instead, it has been *created* by God. Ethics are not autonomous and situational or relative; they have been established by God and are revealed in His Word. Certain things are right and certain things are wrong. There are absolutes, according to the Bible. History is *not* cyclical. It is based upon the providential, sovereign will of Almighty God.

MAN'S REDEMPTION

Man's spiritual rebirth or awakening cannot be achieved by affirming or aligning himself with his supposed divine essence or by cultivating mystical phenomena. A change of consciousness will not save man spiritually. Death for man is *not* an illusion, nor an entrance into the next life form (reincarnation).

Man must receive Jesus Christ as Lord and Savior to know God or have access to Him by prayer: "He who believes in the Son has eternal life; but he who does not obey the Son shall not see life, but the wrath of God abides on him" (John 3:36). The New Age says that through mystical examination and psychic development man can be reconstructed spiritually and emerge as a superior individual. Man, in this viewpoint, is the enthroned controller of his destiny by his response. This teaching is false.

There are two critical danger zones in the New Age. The

first is reincarnation, and the second is channeling or trance channeling.

REINCARNATION

In New Age philosophy man is on an eternal life-cycle plane. Prominent New Agers claim many previous life forms in past centuries, with fantastic stories associated. What a hopeless future if we have to return to this earth that is so trodden down with sin, disease, misery, and pain! Yet this is all that New Agers have to look forward to.

Jesus said, "Do not marvel at this, for an hour is coming in which all who are in the tombs shall hear His voice, and shall come forth: those who did the good deeds to a resurrection of life, those who committed the evil deeds to a resurrection of judgment" (John 5:28,29).

There is no reincarnation, but there is a future judgment, a review of our lives before God (Matthew 12:36).

CHANNELING

In Mark chapter 5 the man of the Gerasenes was totally demon-possessed. The legion of demons used his vocal chords, pronounced discernible words, and spoke out of him (Mark 5:6,9).

We learn from Scripture that demons can invade a human body and possess it. The thought behind demon possession in the New Testament is "demonized." Most often this is associated with a sin problem.

Channeling closely resembles demon-possession. I believe that some people involved in New Age trance-channeling are entertaining demons. Remember, demon-possession does not have to be vomiting, turning green, or some other wild contortion. Demons can convey sweet messages, form peaceful facial expressions, and perform any other kind of tranquility or spiritual discovery in order to lead people further away from Jesus Christ.

But remember, Jesus Christ is returning, and only Jesus Christ can bring about a true new age of peace and power!

13

Protective Petra

◆ ═══════════════════ ◆

He (the Antichrist) will also enter the Beautiful Land, and many countries will fall; but these will be rescued out of his hand: Edom, Moab and the foremost of the sons of Ammon.

—Daniel 11:41

I saw another angel ascending from the rising of the sun, having the seal of the living God; and he cried out with a loud voice to the four angels to whom it was granted to harm the earth and the sea, saying, 'Do not harm the earth or the sea or the trees, until we have sealed the bondservants of our God on their foreheads.' And I heard the number of those who were sealed, one hundred and forty-four thousand sealed from every tribe of the sons of Israel" (Revelation 7:2-4).

When the Antichrist comes to his one-world-government seat of power he will craftily institute his evil, subtle agenda. Initially the Jews will be thrilled with this messiah of peace and incomparable answer-man. He will have spellbinding remedies to many of the problems of the day. The

Jewish nation will be so captured with him that they will establish a covenant with him, according to the centuries-old prophecy of Daniel 9:27.

THE ANTICHRIST'S COVENANT

This covenant will entail many things for the Israelites. Protectively, the Antichrist will umbrella the Israelite nation from the hostilities of their neighboring nations. Miraculously, the Jewish temple will be rebuilt under his reign. This, unquestionably, is the accomplishment of all accomplishments! Achieving this one goal would certainly be enough for every Jew to enthusiastically enthrone this dazzling man as king and dictator.

From our perspective today, the rebuilding of the Jewish temple in the exact spot where foundation stones of the previous one are still visible seems like an impossibility. Yet it will happen.

Obviously, this will be no small task! Its achievement will catapult the Antichrist to far greater preeminence. Yet how he will achieve this milestone is not completely clear. The Dome of the Rock, the highly regarded Muslim temple, sits on the exact stone formation of the ancient Jewish temple. To the Arabs this is a holy and revered spot. Supposedly Mohammed was to have left earth and translated to heaven at this very place.

After Israel won the Six-Day War in June of 1967, the chief rabbinate issued a warning that the Jews should not step inside the temple area, since the Arabs jealously keep guard over this religiously important location. They know that to the Israelites it is highly desired. Why?

At this exact spot on Mt. Moriah thousands of years ago, Abraham was willing to offer up Issac, his son, as a sacrifice of obedience, according to ancient Jewish tradition. All three of the previous temples have been built on this precise location. Somehow the Antichrist will negotiate for a fourth Jewish temple to be rebuilt on these premises early in the tribulation.

Following the construction of the temple, Jewish sacrifice will be reinstituted. What a wonderful, caring man this Antichrist will seem to be! But suddenly in the middle of the seventieth week (the middle of the tribulation) the Antichrist will walk into the temple and proclaim himself God!

WORSHIP OR FLEE

He will demand that he alone be worshiped. Don't forget that he will attempt to authenticate his claim to deity by healing himself of a mortal wound. "He [the false prophet] exercises all the authority of the first beast in his presence. And he makes the earth and those who dwell in it to worship the first beast, whose fatal wound was healed" (Revelation 13:12).

Via satellite television the whole world will behold in wondrous amazement the Antichrist's self-healing. "He is not a man, he must be God," humanity will breathe in unison. Many of the Jews in spite of this most blasphemous act in the temple will follow the Antichrist.

However, God's Word clearly reveals that the remnant of the nation of Israel, previously marked by an angel of God, will have their eyes opened. Immediately they will flee!

According to Revelation 7:2-8 at least 144,000 Jewish people, representative of the 12 tribes of Israel will flee for their lives.

Sequentially, this is where Matthew 24:16-22 fits, speaking to the exiting Jews daring to survive, insubordinate to the Antichrist: "Then let those who are in Judea flee to the mountains; let him who is on the housetop not go down to get the things out that are in his house; and let him who is in the field not turn back to get his cloak. But woe to those who are with child and to those who nurse babes in those days! But pray that your flight may not be in the winter, or on a Sabbath; for then there will be a great tribulation, such as has not occurred since the beginning of the world until now, nor ever shall. And unless those days had been cut short, no life would have been saved; but for the sake of the elect those days shall be cut short."

SAFE HAVEN IN THE ROCK

Where will these thousands of Jews be fleeing? Many Bible teachers believe it to be the ancient city of Petra, hewn out of solid rock, and still existing today.

Interestingly, Petra is located in one of the three countries which Daniel 11:41 indicates will escape the tyranny of the Antichrist. Note these words: "These will be rescued out of his hand: Edom" (Daniel 11:41). The city of Petra is located in biblical Edom. Edom in history goes back to the Genesis record that declares Esau to be Edom: "Esau said to Jacob, 'Please let me have a swallow of that red stuff there, for I am famished.' Therefore his name was called Edom" (Genesis 25:30).

Edom is a specific land south of Jerusalem, and Petra is located in the mountains of Edom. According to Bible prophecy, when the Antichrist begins to terrorize the Jews in dictatorial frenzy, Edom is to escape out of his control.

Petra is located almost due south of the Dead Sea and slightly northeast of the Gulf of Aqaba. What a fortress it is! Uniquely, it is a city carved out of solid rock. It even has a great amphitheater, seating 3000, also carved out of rock by the Romans in the second century A.D.

Numerous Bible teachers believe that two verses of Scripture relate to the Israelites hiding in Petra.

First, Revelation 12:6: "And the woman [Israel] fled into the wilderness, where she had a place prepared by God, so that there she might be nourished for one thousand two hundred and sixty days."

Second, Revelation 12:14: "And the two wings of the great eagle were given to the woman [Israel], in order that she might fly into the wilderness *to her place*, where she was nourished for a time and times and half a time, from the presence of the serpent."

"One thousand two hundred and sixty days" and a "time [one year] and times [two years] and half a time [six months]" equals exactly 3½ years in duration. Revelation 13:5 reminds us that this is the exact time period of the Antichrist's abhorrent rule in the Great Tribulation.

There certainly is scriptural suggestion that Petra will be the place for the housing of the remnant of escaping Israelites during the last half of the tribulation period.

DIVINE PROTECTION

The question might be asked, "Why won't the Antichrist exterminate the fleeing Jews as they head south for refuge?" Revelation 12:16 answers: "The earth helped the woman [Israel], and the earth opened its mouth and drank up the river [soldiers] which the dragon poured out of his mouth."

Somewhere along the way to southern Petra the earth will open its mouth, devouring the pursuing Antichrist armies. The main force back in Jerusalem will have no reason to further attack the remnant of Israel, who will be shut up inside the ancient stone city of Petra.

"Come, my people, enter into your rooms, and close your doors behind you; hide for a little while, until indignation runs its course. For behold, the Lord is about to come out from His place to punish the inhabitants of the earth for their inquity; and the earth will reveal her bloodshed, and will no longer cover her slain" (Isaiah 26:20,21).

How will the Israelites be fed for 3½ years? "... where she had a place prepared by God, so that there she might be nourished for one thousand two hundred and sixty days" (Revelation 12:6). God will supply her needs and preserve her until the second coming of Jesus Christ, perhaps in a similiar way to the manna afforded to the Israelites for 40 years in the blistering wilderness.

Due to divine decree the protected Jews will live to the coming of Jesus Christ. Petra ... what an arresting thought of God's protection in the most troubled of times!

14

The Battle of Blood

◆ ══════════════ ◆

They gathered them together to the place which in Hebrew is called Har-Magedon.

—Revelation 16:16

I saw heaven opened; and behold, a white horse, and He who sat upon it is called Faithful and True; and in righteousness He judges and wages war. And His eyes are a flame of fire, and upon His head are many diadems; and He has a name written upon Him which no one knows except Himself. And He is clothed with a robe dipped in blood; and His name is called The Word of God. And the armies which are in heaven, clothed in fine linen, white and clean, were following Him on white horses. And from His mouth comes a sharp sword, so that with it He may smite the nations; and He will rule them with a rod of iron; and He treads the winepress of the fierce wrath of God, the Almighty. And on His robe and on His thigh He has a name written, 'KING OF KINGS AND LORD OF LORDS.' And I saw an angel standing in the sun; and he cried out with a loud voice, saying to all the birds which fly in midheaven,

'Come, assemble for the great supper of God; in order that you may eat the flesh of kings and the flesh of commanders and the flesh of mighty men and the flesh of horses and of those who sit on them and the flesh of all men, both free men and slaves, and small and great.' And I saw the beast and the kings of the earth and their armies, assembled to make war against Him who sat upon the horse, and against His army" (Revelation 19:11-19).

"And the rest were killed with the sword which came from the mouth of Him who sat upon the horse, and all the birds were filled with their flesh" (Revelation 19:21).

THE FINAL BATTLE

There have been many battles in the history of mankind, but none can compare to the battle of blood which will culminate the Great Tribulation.

As the Antichrist mounts his power post he will bring the majority of nations under his command. But even the Antichrist will have difficulty getting allegiance from every country. Daniel's prophecy is especially pertinent here:

At the end time the king of the South will collide with him, and the king of the North will storm against him with chariots, with horsemen, and with many ships; and he will enter countries, overflow them, and pass through. He will also enter the Beautiful Land, and many countries will fall; but these will be rescued out of his hand: Edom, Moab and the foremost of the sons of Ammon. Then he will stretch out his hand against other countries, and the land of Egypt will not escape. But he will gain control over the hidden treasures of gold and silver, and over all the precious things of Egypt; and Libyans and Ethiopians will follow at his heels. But rumors from the East and from the North will disturb him, and he will go forth with great wrath to destroy and annihilate many. And he will pitch the tents of his royal pavilion between the seas and the beautiful Holy Mountain, yet he will come to his end, and no one will help him" (Daniel 11:40-45).

The king of the North seems to be Russia. The kings of the East are China. This most populous nation boasts an army exceeding 200 million! For years critics of the Bible scoffed at Revelation 9:16, "And the number of the armies of the horsemen was two hundred million; I heard the number of them." Possibly Japan will be united with China in a march of defiance and war against the Antichrist.

According to Daniel, the Antichrist enters and sets up headquarters in the Beautiful Land. This is a reference to Israel. Other Scriptures remind us that the Antichrist will be operating in Jerusalem.

But he will have trouble on his hands. Armies from the east and north will descend down upon him. The Beast will have a whole contingent of hundreds of millions of men with their military arsenals under his direction.

Jesus' Olivet Discourse indicates that there will be wars and rumors of wars throughout the tribulation right up to the moment of Christ's second coming to the world (see Matthew 24:6). There will be battles and conflagrations during the tribulation, especially the last 3$\frac{1}{2}$ years.

Some Bible teachers think the United States is symbolized through the appearance of Babylon in Revelation chapter 18. This eerie chapter proclaims her death in one hour! The language seems to speak of a nuclear attack devastating the nation to ashes: "For this reason in one day her plagues will come, pestilence and mourning and famine, and she will be burned up with fire; for the Lord God who judges her is strong" (Revelation 18:8).

It sends chills up my back . . . maybe America is destroyed by a nuclear holocaust prior to the end-all battle, Armageddon. The United States destroyed? Could it possibly be?

IMPENDING JUDGMENT

Our country is sinning in spite of the great spiritual light that God has shed upon us. Once the great universities of America had a Christian foundation, but now God is relegated outside. The first textbook in our public schools was the Bible, but now it would be easier for me to use profanity on a high school platform than to mention the name of the Lord Jesus Christ!

Why would America be destroyed? "To the degree that she glorified herself and lived sensuously, to the same degree give her torment and mourning; for she says in her heart, 'I sit as a queen and I am not a widow, and will never see mourning'" (Revelation 18:7).

Wherever America is, the Battle of Armageddon is sure to ensue. The Battle is at the very end of the tribulation period, detailed in Revelation chapters 6 through 19.

Prior to this point the earth has staggered under the multiple judgments leveled by God. As Revelation chapter 6 opens, in verses 1 and 2 we see the Antichrist going forth "conquering, and to conquer." Peace is immediately and permanently taken from the earth: "And another, a red horse, went out; and to him who sat on it, it was granted to take peace from the earth, and that men should slay one another; and a great sword was given to him" (Revelation 6:4).

You think the murder rate is bad now, with one homicide every 24 minutes; wait until the tribulation begins! Killing will become too common a thing to report on the evening news.

Famine will have strangled the lives of millions worldwide. According to Revelation 6:5,6 it will take a man's entire day's pay to feed his family one meal. This indicates that rationing will be commonplace during the tribulation. So great will the famine be that Revelation 6:7,8 informs us that one-fourth of earth's life will die.

Martyrdom will be the only choice for those who decide to make Christ Lord of their life during the tribulation. Revelation 6:9-11 suggests that many will face the guillotine because they have rejected the mark of the Beast.

Recently a young man questioned me regarding these tribulation martyrs. He sincerely thought that no one would be saved after the rapture of the church and commencement of the tribulation. But this text and Revelation 7:9-17 make it perfectly clear that many will come to Christ during the tribulation.

The earthquakes mentioned in Revelation 6:12-17 may be the result of a nuclear exchange. It will be so hideous that thousands of people will be screaming to die to end the pain. There will be atmospheric changes, and the climates will be dramatically altered.

We have so many nuclear bombs on this planet right now that one physicist calculates that the total is equivalent to 10 tons of TNT for every living person on earth!

As the nations of the earth converge to fight one another, Christ will suddenly return. Suddenly the guns of the world will turn on Jesus Christ. Perhaps the buttons of hundreds of nuclear bombs will be pushed—but Jesus Christ will conquer the world!

15

The Awaiting Glory

◆ ══════════════════════ ◆

I saw a new heaven and a new earth; for the first heaven and the first earth passed away, and there is no longer any sea. And I saw the holy city, new Jerusalem, coming down out of heaven from God, made ready as a bride adorned for her husband. And I heard a loud voice from the throne, saying, "Behold, the tabernacle of God is among men, and He shall dwell among them, and they shall be His people, and God Himself shall be among them, and He shall wipe away every tear from their eyes; and there shall no longer be any death; there shall no longer be any mourning, or crying, or pain; the first things have passed away.

—Revelation 21:1-4

No movie created in Hollywood has ever made the impact on audiences worldwide as did Steven Spielberg's heartwarming masterpiece of love between a young boy and an alien visitor from outer space entitled "E.T."—the Extra-Terrestrial.

Filled with unparalleled magic and imagination that

made audiences around the world laugh and cry, E.T. follows the moving story of a lost little alien befriended by a ten-year-old boy named Elliot. The unforgettable, classic statement by the homesick, out-of-place alien, E.T., was PHONE HOME. He longed to return to his true home, for he was disoriented and potentially dissected by fearful, inquisitive humans.

What a classic illustration to every one of us as Christians that we live in a foreign world that is not our permanent home! Peter refers to us as "aliens and strangers" in this world (1 Peter 2:11). Let's take a moment and "phone home." We are going to get an incredibly invigorating picture of our future priceless home called *heaven*.

PREPARING FOR ETERNITY

By the way...are you prepared for eternity? Are you prepared to die? We often think of death as something quite distant and remote. However, one thing is certain— we are all going to die! Where will you go after you die? Nowhere does Scripture teach extinction or soul sleep. There are literal places after death, but none is as glorious as heaven.

The population of the world is now over five billion. The United Nations has estimated that about 11 percent of the population dies each year. Today alone, over 130,000 people throughout the world will die. Where are you going? Where are all these millions of passing people going?

The Bible refers to heaven approximately 550 times. In the Old Testament the Hebrew word translated "heaven" is plural and literally means "the heights." The Greek word for heaven in the New Testament is *ouranos*, which inspired the name of the planet Uranus. The word refers to that which is raised up or lofty.

Newsweek magazine conducted a very interesting religious poll; they asked how many Americans believe in God. A startling 94 percent stated a firm belief that God exists. Furthermore, 77 percent of Americans polled said they believed in heaven. And among the 77 percent, three out of four people rated their chances of getting there "good" or "excellent."

Conversely, the ominous warning from the lips of Jesus Christ was, "For the gate is small, and the way is narrow that leads to life, and *few* are those who find it" (Matthew 7:14).

The word "heaven" is extremely popular. Yet shockingly, much of the preaching today largely ignores heaven. You can count on one hand the number of sermons a person can hear in his or her entire lifetime on heaven. Why? A materialistic world and satanic forces deliberately disguise the glory that is ahead for those who truly know Christ.

It is often those who are suffering or near death's door who appreciate the thought of heaven the most. Suffering uniquely prepares us for heaven and consoles us that there is a better place waiting for us.

Dr. Francis Patton (1843-1932), a former president of Princeton University, observed that whereas the high-water mark of the Old Testament was Psalm 23:4, "Even though I walk through the valley of the shadow of death, I will fear no evil," that of the New Testament was Philippians 1:23, where Paul said, "But I am hard-pressed from both directions, having the desire to depart and be with Christ, for that is very much better." David was willing to go but wanting to stay; Paul was willing to stay but wanting to go!

How much more would we want to go to heaven if we took the time to realize what God has prepared for us there!

The classic allegory *Pilgrim's Progress* presents the central character, Pilgrim, a disguise for Bunyan himself. Pilgrim was totally obsessed to get to the heavenly city.

Driven to enter the land of no sorrow, Pilgrim let all other pursuits fall by the wayside. Even Pilgrim's closest friends considered him eccentric. Mr. Obstinate declared that Pilgrim was "brainsick" and "crazy-headed." But Pilgrim wanted to make sure he was going to be in heaven someday.

I have often said to my wife of those individuals displaying great wealth and boasting of no need for God that they *better enjoy it now*, because it is all they are ever going to have!

THE THREEFOLD HEAVENS

The word "heaven" is used in many different ways today. Of the Bible's 550 verses with the word "heaven" in them, three different definitions are conveyed.

Sometimes the appearance of "heaven" simply means the *atmosphere*, the air we breathe. Isaiah 55:9 says, "For as the heavens are higher than the earth...."

In some occurrences the term "heaven" indicated the astral system: "God said, 'Let there be an expanse in the midst of the waters'" (Genesis 1:6).

Often the term "heaven" in Scripture refers to the location of God's throne. This is the case in Revelation chapters 21 and 22 (see also Isaiah 57:15). Jesus repeatedly stressed that the Father was in *heaven*: "Let your light shine before men in such a way that they may see your good works and glorify your Father who is in heaven" (Matthew 5:16). "For whoever does the will of My Father who is in heaven, he is My brother and sister and mother" (Matthew 12:50). "See that you do not despise one of these little ones, for I say to you that their angels in heaven continually behold the face of My Father who is in heaven" (Matthew 18:10).

Jesus promised heaven for those who followed Him. Though heaven is a state, it is also a place! No one emphasized this any stronger than Christ: "Let not your heart be troubled; believe in God, believe also in Me. In My Father's house are many dwelling *places*; if it were not so, I would have told you; for I go to prepare a *place* for you. And if I go and prepare a *place* for you, I will come again and receive you to Myself, that where I am, there you may be also" (John 14:1-3).

Three times Jesus used the term "place." Heaven is a literal place, just as real as New York or Los Angeles, but infinitely better. Heaven is as real and literal as the concrete in your home and the city limit sign of your town.

A GLIMPSE OF HEAVEN

Paul, the greatest Christian who ever lived and was decapitated for Christ, was allowed a premature glimpse of heaven. It was a closely guarded secret for Paul. And many Christians are unaware of Paul's rapturous trip to the celestial city. "I know a man in Christ who fourteen years ago—whether in the body I do not know, or out of the body I do not know, God knows—such a man was caught up to the third heaven. And I know how such a man—whether in the body or apart from the body I do not know, God knows—was caught up into Paradise, and heard inexpressible words, which a man is not permitted to speak" (2 Corinthians 12:2-4).

Notice verse 2: "fourteen years ago"...that was when Paul took his first itinerant preaching journey in approximately 46 A.D. Most scholars agree that Paul wrote the second letter to the church in Corinth in 60 A.D. Reflecting back to the physical agony of what happened in the city of

Lystra when an angry, incited mob stoned Paul, he was apparently left for dead on the outskirts of town. Even the mob left Paul under a mountain of stones, no doubt assuming he was dead. And he probably was! (See Acts 14:19.) In this precise moment Paul was caught up to heaven and given a premature excursion of the beautiful city.

Verse 2 says he was "caught up." In the Greek this is a term which expresses removal from one place to another without the agency of the subject. The verb means the swift, resistless, impetuous seizure of spiritual ecstasy (also found in Acts 8:39 and 1 Thessalonians 4:17). God removed Paul temporarily from earth's dismal cloud of tears, persecution, and torment.

In verse 4 Paul says he was caught up into paradise. Noted theologian Charles Hodge calls this the highest heaven. The word in Greek means a "beautiful park" or "garden," similar to Eden in Genesis 2:8. It is the exact same word that Jesus used to reassure the repentant dying thief in Luke 23:43.

What actually did Paul see? He says he heard "inexpressible" words. Since technically there is no such thing as "unspeakable" or "inexpressible" words, we call this an "oxymoron," a combination of contradictory terms intended to convey something in human terms which is unfathomable.

"The veil which concealed the mysteries and glories of heaven God has not permitted to be raised," related Charles Hodge. "No doubt no human language could describe the glory. It would have been like trying to picture a sunset to a man born blind," commented Henrietta Mears. "Paul's humble character is revealed here. We have the rarest of all examples: a boastless boast! He had kept this a secret for 14 years. It is now forced from him only by necessity. Most men would have written several volumes on such an experience or given a whole series of messages. But this is all that Paul says. He says so much and yet he says so little. There is no Chamber of Commerce advertisement, no promotion, no sales talk, no display, no hero worship," writes J. Vernon McGee.

Applicable to the thought of heaven is 1 Corinthians 2:9: "Things which eye has not seen and ear has not heard, and which have not entered the heart of man, all that God has prepared for those who love Him." We have never seen, experienced, or heard what will compare to the utter glory of heaven. However, God has given us a foretaste by His Spirit and abundant life on the way to heaven.

In Revelation chapters 21 and 22 we have a new heaven, a new earth, a new people, a new light, a new temple, and a new city.

HEAVEN: PLACE OF PERFECT PURITY

"Nothing unclean and no one who practices abomination and lying shall ever come into it, but only those whose names are written in the Lamb's book of life" (Revelation 21:27). Heaven is a place of absolute perfect purity. Think of it! There is no impurity whatsoever in this heavenly city. Even the street of the city is paved with pure gold. The gold we know of is often stained and clouded, but the street of the city is paved with *pure* gold. What John saw must have sparkled with a brilliance and glow that had a golden tone but was still brilliantly clear.

There will be no more *curse* in the heavenly city: "There shall no longer be any curse" (Revelation 22:3). We are used to living in a world where everything shows the curse of man's rebellion against God. When Adam fell in disobedience from God, our world fell, and the curse has been passed by birth from one generation to the next. God said to Adam, "Cursed is the ground because of you; in toil you shall eat of it all the days of your life" (Genesis 3:17).

Man is born crying and he dies crying. The wind whistles in a minor key. For every rose bloom there is a stem with thorns. For every joy there is a sorrow. For every sunshine there is a storm. And everywhere you look you see the mark of the curse. But in that day the curse will be lifted! "For I consider that the sufferings of this present time are not worthy to be compared with the glory that is to be revealed to us" (Romans 8:18).

There will be no more *defilement* in the heavenly city: "Outside are the dogs and the sorcerers and the immoral persons and the murderers and the idolaters, and everyone who loves and practices lying" (Revelation 22:15). The National Coalition Against Domestic Violence reports that a woman is battered by her husband or boyfriend in this country every 15 seconds, making domestic violence America's most common but least reported crime.[1] Happily, there will be no more battering and abusing in heaven!

Sandy Rodriguez was 12 years old and stood at four feet, five inches. Ravaged by the AIDS virus, she weighed a meager 40 pounds. Before her death in a New Jersey hospital she pleaded, "Dear God, this is Sandy. Please help me, God. Help me, please. I don't want to hurt anymore. I'm scared." The recipient of a contaminated blood transfusion, Sandy suffered pitifully to the day of her death. Her mom was a drug addict who had long since overdosed, leaving Sandy diseased and awaiting death.

Before her death she said to the nurse, "You go to God. I can walk there. No pain in my stomach, no pain in my knee. I can walk again." Yes, Sandy will be shouting down the streets of the eternal city which has no defilement.

The scenario for earth is much more grim. The World Health Organization says that at least 10 million children will likely be infected with the AIDS virus by the year 2000!

But Peter says to us about our future home, "To obtain an inheritance which is imperishable and undefiled and will not fade away, reserved in heaven for you" (1 Peter 1:4).

There will be no more *darkness* in the heavenly city. This is good news: The darkness of this world will vanish forever. In the Bible darkness is equated with evil. Darkness brings with it loneliness. During the recent war with Iraq, many wives of absent GI's made it through the day fine, but at night, when the shadows lengthened, the loneliness and emptiness pounded on their minds and emotions merlessly.

When I was a kid I always wanted my dad and mom to :ave the hall light on at night. I'll always remember the hill of fear that seemed to creep into every inch of my oom, enveloping me when the hall light was off. I hated the larkness. And now, with my little lad Jeremy, I gladly leave he hall light on!

Praise God, in our new city darkness is an unknown quality. Revelation 21:23 says, "The city has no need of the sun or of the moon to shine upon it, for the glory of God has illumined it, and its lamp is the Lamb." See also Revelation 21:25 and 22:5.

HEAVEN: PLACE OF PERFECT POPULATION

Who will be in heaven? "You have come to Mount Zion and to the city of the living God, the heavenly Jerusalem, and to myriads of angels, to the general assembly and church of the firstborn who are enrolled in heaven, and to God, the Judge of all, and to the spirits of righteous men made perfect, and to Jesus, the mediator of a new covenant" (Hebrews 12:22-24).

Who will be there? God, innumerable angels, Christians of all the ages, and Old Testament believers. This will be a reunion of all reunions!

"Those who have insight will shine brightly like the brightness of the expanse of heaven, and those who lead the many to righteousness like the stars forever and ever" (Daniel 12:3). Jesus said in Matthew 8:11, "I say unto you that many shall come from east and west, and recline at the table with Abraham and Isaac and Jacob in the kingdom of heaven."

We will know our loved ones in heaven. Forever we will retain our image and identity: "For now we see in a mirror dimly, but then face to face; now I know in part, but then I shall know fully, just as I also have been fully known" (1 Corinthians 13:12). The simplest yet most profound illustration of this was Jesus Christ at what is commonly called the Mount of Transfiguration: "He was transfigured before them; and His face shone like the sun, and His garments became as white as light. And behold, Moses and Elijah appeared to them, talking with Him" (Matthew 17:2,3). Notice that Moses and Elijah appeared with recognizable identities even after centuries in heaven.

Will we marry in heaven? According to the Bible, heaven will offer a wondrously superior form of life from that of earth: "In the resurrection they neither marry nor are given in marriage, but are like angels in heaven" (Matthew 22:30). Paul said, "The form of this world is passing away" (1 Corinthians 7:31b). Marriage will be obsolete; there will be a different heavenly lifestyle, and it will be marvelous!

HEAVEN: PLACE OF PERFECT PEACE

"He [God] shall wipe away every tear from their eyes" (Revelation 21:4). This is one of the most tender passages in the entire Bible. There will be *no tears* in the heavenly city. As we walk down the golden streets, we will be looking through eyes which will no longer cry. We will no longer even remember what sorrow was. "Weeping may last for the night, but a shout of joy comes in the morning" (Psalm 30:5).

There will be *no sickness* in the heavenly city. Our bodies will be at their zenith of capability, untouched by the limitation of sin. "There shall no longer be any . . . pain" (Revelation 21:4). "Who will transform the body of our humble state into conformity with the body of His glory" (Philippians 3:21). "Just as we have borne the image of the earthly, we shall also bear the image of the heavenly" (1 Corinthians 15:49).

Jesus after the resurrection was a classic example of what the glorified body will be like. He suddenly appeared in rooms where doors were shut (John 20:19,26). In heaven our souls and bodies will be eternally perfect.

HEAVEN: PLACE OF PERFECT PROVISION

Interestingly, the heavenly city is built on a great river, as are many of our earthly cities, such as Rome, Paris, Tel Aviv, and London. But those rivers are filthy with contamination. The heavenly river is as pure as crystal as it proceeds out of the throne of God.

"He showed me a river of the water of life, clear as crystal, coming from the throne of God" (Revelation 22:1). "I will give to the one who thirsts from the spring of the water of life without cost" (Revelation 21:6b).

So there will be *drinking* and *eating* in heaven! "On either side of the river was the tree of life, bearing twelve kinds of fruit, yielding its fruit every month; and the leaves of the tree were for the healing of the nations" (Revelation 22:2). In heaven we will eat for pure enjoyment. The Greek word for "healing" is *therapeia*, from which we get the English word "therapeutic." John is saying that the leaves of the tree of life promote the enrichment of life. This heavenly food will exhilarate us celestially, and the water of life is for the sheer joy of drinking.

HEAVEN: PLACE OF PERFECT PROPORTIONS

The verse is very clear to understand: "The city is laid out as a square, and its length is as great as the width; and he measured the city with the rod, fifteen hundred miles; its length and width and height are equal" (Revelation 21:16).

There is no city on earth that can even begin to compare to our future enormous heavenly city. We can behold the city we are stunned with, a city that has walls of jasper 250 feet high. Jasper in the Bible is a diamond-colored stone. There is no way to calculate how much 250-foot walls of diamond would be worth. The Bible says the city will be 1500 miles in *every direction—high, wide,* and *long.* This is breathtaking, to say the least!

The heavenly city will be so Gargantuan that it would stretch from Maine to Florida or from New York City to Colorado.

Yes, the heavenly city is enormous; it will have hundreds of levels and thousands of intersecting golden avenues. Life will be lavish and unspeakably glorious. It will be intricately complex in our ongoing learning of God and His never-ending creation.

Augustus Strong said, "Cities are more than masses of population; they are citadels for mutual safety, conduits of commercial enterprise, and centers for artistic and scientific creativity. The representation of heaven as a city was intended to suggest intensity of life, variety of occupation, and closeness of relation to each other."

HEAVEN: PLACE OF PERFECT PLEASURE

Revelation 11:15 says: "He will reign forever and ever." However, Revelation 22:5 rings out, "and *they* shall reign forever and ever."

We as believers in Christ will *reign with Him*: "Everyone who has left houses or brothers or sisters or father or mother or children or farms for My name's sake shall receive many times as much, and shall inherit eternal life" (Matthew 19:29). Reinforcing this thought is Revelation 5:10: "Thou hast made them to be a kingdom and priests to our God; and they will reign upon the earth."

Commenting on Luke 19:12-19 (the men given different talents by the Lord), noted Bible scholar William Evans presents the following thoughts. "As men differ in their commitment to Christ, in their fidelity, zeal, and labor, so they differ in spiritual gains and rewards (10 cities, 5 cities, etc.). The reward (reigning position) of the believer will be in proportion to the faithfulness of his service for God with the use of the talents with which God has endowed him. The rewards, therefore, will differ according to the faithfulness or unfaithfulness of our service or life. Faith in Jesus Christ saves the believer, but his position in the future life together with the measure of his reward will depend upon his faithfulness in the use of the gifts with which he has been endowed by God."

In heaven we will *serve Him*: "The throne of God and of the Lamb shall be in it, and His bondservants shall serve Him" (Revelation 22:3). I believe that Adam in the Garden of Eden prior to his sinful disobedience is a clear picture of us someday in heaven. Adam was serving God by tending after the garden, but the work was enjoyable. There weren't even any weeds!

In heaven we will *see Him.* "They shall see His face, and His name shall be on their foreheads" (Revelation 22:4). Moses, after his trip to Mount Sinai, radiated with God's glory. In heaven we will see Him. Like Thomas, we will touch Him. We will sit with Him and sing with Him. We will have perfect knowledge in heaven.

In heaven we will *worship Him.* I believe in praise here on this side of heaven. Why? Because we will be praising and worshiping God forever in the land where the sun never sets. Never will I forget when I sat in the RAI Center in Amsterdam and listened to nearly 8000 evangelists praying and praising God in hundreds of different languages. They were there from all over the globe, attending the Billy Graham International Conference for Itinerant Evangelists. It was like a beehive.

In heaven our beehive of praise will never stop! Jesus promised, "Blessed are the pure in heart, for they shall see God" (Matthew 5:8). We will be singing in heaven. That picture is repeatedly presented in Revelation and other places of the Scripture. "In Thy presence is fullness of joy; in Thy right hand there are pleasures forever" (Psalm 16:11).

Charles Fuller once announced that he would be speaking the following Sunday on heaven. During the week he received a beautiful letter from an old man who was very ill. The following is part of his letter to Charles Fuller:

Next Sunday you are to talk on heaven. I am very interested in that land, because I have held a clear title to a bit of property there for over 55 years. I did not buy it. It was given to me without money and without price. But the donor purchased it for me at a tremendous sacrifice. I am not holding it for speculation, since the title is not transferable. It is not a vacant lot.

For more than half a century I have been sending materials out of which the greatest architect and builder of the universe has been building a home for me which will never need to be remodeled or repaired because it will suit me perfectly and individually, and will never grow old.

Termites can never undermine its foundations, for they rest on the Rock of Ages. Fire cannot destroy it. Floods cannot wash it away. No person can ever enter that land where my dwelling stands, now almost completed and almost ready for me to enter in and abide in peace eternally, without fear of being ejected.

There is a valley of deep shadow between the place where I live in California and that to which I shall journey in a very short time. I cannot reach my home in that city of God without passing through this dark valley of shadows. But I am not afraid because the best friend I ever had went through the same valley long, long ago and drove away all its gloom. He has stuck by me through thick and thin, since we first became acquainted fifty-five years ago, and I hold His promise in printed form, never to forsake me or leave me alone. He will be with me as I walk through the valley of shadows, and I shall not lose my way when He is with me.

I hope to hear your sermon on heaven next Sunday from my home in Los Angeles, California, but I have no assurance that I shall be able to do so. My ticket to heaven has no date marked for the journey, no return coupon, and no permit for baggage. Yes, I am all ready to go and I may not be here while you are talking next Sunday evening, but I shall meet you there someday.

Are your bags packed? Are you prepared for this ultimate journey? In light of current events and God's prophetic Word, it has never been more important that we be ready. May He find you standing at the station anticipating His return.

Appendices

◆ ══════════════════════ ◆

The Greats Sound Off!
Notes
Glossary of Terms

The Greats Sound Off!

◆ ════════════ ◆

The theme of the second coming of Christ has galvanized the greatest minds in Christendom with expectation. God has raised up men and women who have blown the trumpet to wake up mankind to the inescapable fact that Jesus Christ is returning to planet Earth! As I study the biblical teaching of end times, my faith is strengthened by these spiritual giants who have sounded the warning. Though they lived in different times, their challenge of the imminent return of Christ is the same. We do well to heed their exhortation and live *every day* in expectation of Christ's return.

One of my favorite writers on the subject of eschatology is Dr. John Walvoord. Listen to his comments on the nations of the East.

> One of the important developments of the twentieth century is the rising power of Oriental countries such as Red China, Japan, and India. The release of these major countries from foreign domination and their growing importance from the military and economic standpoint has reversed a trend of centuries. It is obvious that in future world affairs, the Orient will increase in importance. Its multiplied millions of souls, its large territorial area, and its potential for economic and political development are obvious to all observers.
>
> From the standpoint of Biblical prophecy, the Orient is important because of certain prophecies which indicate its participation in events at the end of the age. In the Scriptures which describe the final world conflict, including a gigantic world war, one of the military forces is described as coming out of the East. The ruler of Daniel 11:36-45 is troubled by "tidings out of the east," apparently an indication of rebellion against him and military attacks from the East. This is given further light in the book of Revelation, where in chapter 9, in connection with the sounding of the

sixth trumpet, an army is described as coming from the East from the great river Euphrates numbering 200 million and capable of slaying a third part of the earth's population (Revelation 9:15,16). A later development of this matter is given prominence in the sixth vial of Revelation 16:12-16, where it is predicted that the Euphrates River will be dried up "that the way of kings of the east might be prepared."[1]

Charles Hodge made an indelible mark on his 3000 students at Princeton University. He is viewed as one of the great theologians of the Christian church. Hodge was a powerful conservative force in the Presbyterian Church in the mid-1800's.

In Romans 11:25 (For I do not want you, brethren, to be uninformed of this mystery, lest you be wise in your own estimation, that a partial hardening has happened to Israel until the fulness of the Gentiles has come in) Paul teaches that the national conversion of the Jews is not to take place "until the fulness of the Gentiles be come in." [It] is that which makes the number of Gentiles full, the full complement which the Gentiles are to render to make the number of the elect complete. This ingathering of the heathen is the special work of the Church. It is a missionary work. It was so understood by the Apostles. Their two great duties were the propagation and defense of the truth. To these they devoted themselves. While they labored night and day, and travelled hither and thither through all parts of the Roman world, preaching the Gospel, they labored no less assiduously in its defense. All the epistles of the New Testament, those of Paul, Peter, John, and James, are directed toward the correction of false doctrine. These two duties of propagating and of defending the truth the Apostles devolved on their successors.[2]

Dr. J. Oliver Buswell, chosen the third President of Wheaton College in 1926 until 1940, and later Dean of the Graduate Faculty at Covenant College and Seminary in St. Louis, comments on the term "generation."

All three synoptic Gospels follow the parable of the trees with a reference to "this generation" given in almost identical words. "Truly I say to you, this generation will not pass away until all these things take place" (Matthew 24:34). The word translated "generation," *genea*, primarily means "a begetting." Thayer, Liddell and Scott, and Moulton and Milligan all give such meanings as "people," "race," "family," "kind" before noting any such definition as "contemporaries living at one time." Walter Bauer's *German Worterbuch zum Neuen Testament* gives "geschlecht" (kind or species) as the first definition of *genea*.

It would seem quite obvious that the primary meaning of the Greek word *genea*, translated "generation," namely, "race" or "people," is the meaning to be understood in the passage. The disciples had asked Him about the destruction of the temple. Jesus with His disciples [was] seated on the Mount of Olives looking across the valley directly to the temple area and to the city of Jerusalem. The very words "this generation" suggest a gesture of the hand, pointing to the city and the temple which lay over against them, directly in their view (Mark 13:3). The preservation of the Jewish people through all the intervening centuries since the time of Christ is indeed a remarkable fulfillment of this prophecy.[3]

Dr. William Evans, born in Liverpool, England, in 1870, was later esteemed as one of the foremost Bible teachers in the United States. He is well-known for his volume *The Great Doctrines of the Bible*. Commenting on Jerusalem, he has this to say:

Its history goes back 4000 years to Melchizedek, Genesis 14:17-20. It is mentioned well over 1000 times under its various names. Often destroyed, it has risen from its ashes to continue its astonishing world influence. There Christ was crucified and resurrected, and there the Holy Spirit descended to inaugurate the age of the church.

God made and fashioned the site long ago, Isaiah 22:11, placed it "in the midst of the nations and countries that are round about," Ezekiel 5:5, and chose it for His habitation,

Psalm 132:13. There His glory dwelt, and will one day return, when the millennial temple is erected, Ezekiel 11:23; 43:2.

The times of the Gentiles are said to be fulfilled when they no longer control the city, Luke 21:24. Gentile times will end when Christ reigns from Jerusalem, Zephaniah 3:14-17. The holy city is to become a source of worldwide trouble in the last days, Zechariah 12:2,3. All nations will gather against it to battle, Zechariah 14:2. The Lord will return and deliver the city, Zechariah 14:3,4.

During the kingdom age it is to be the world metropolis from which Christ will rule all nations, Jeremiah 3:17; Isaiah 24:23. It will be elevated above the countryside; from it will flow a great river, Zechariah 14:8-10. Rejoicing will fill the streets of the city, Jeremiah 33:1-16. It will be the joy of the whole earth, Psalm 48:2.[4]

One pastor in North America whom I deeply admire and respect is Dr. W.A. Criswell of the historic First Baptist Church of Dallas, Texas. How will Christ come? He answers:

There are three elements concerning the return of the Lord which we should keep in mind. First, he is coming actually, literally, visibly, openly, bodily, physically. Second, he shall reign over an actual, visible, literal kingdom. Third, we shall be citizens of that kingdom as actual, physical, resurrected, immortalized, glorified people.

We have previously discussed the Greek word that is used in the New Testament for the return of the Lord, that word *parousia*. And we have stressed that this very common word has one meaning, and one meaning only. It denotes a physical, bodily presence. In no place, in no passage, in no example is it, nor can it ever be, used figuratively or spiritually. The word *parousia* refers to a physical, bodily presence.

True enough, the disciples asked him, "What shall be the sign of thy coming [*parousia*]?" and the Lord told them, "For as lightning cometh out of the east, and shineth even unto the west, so shall also the coming [*parousia*] of the Son of man be" (Matthew 24:3,27).[5]

The man who led gang leader Nicky Cruz to Christ, and who now pastors Times Square Church in New York City, said:

> America is going to be destroyed by fire! Sudden destruction is coming, and few will escape. Unexpectedly, and in one hour, a hydrogen holocaust will engulf America—and this nation will be no more.
>
> It is because America has sinned against the greatest light. Other nations are just as sinful, but none are as flooded with gospel light as ours. God is going to judge America for its violence, its crime, its backsliding, its murdering of millions of babies, its flaunting of homosexuality and sadomasochism, its corruption, its drunkenness and drug abuse, its form of godliness without power, its lukewarmness toward Christ, its rampant divorce and adultery, its lewd pornography, its child molestations, its cheating, its robbings, its dirty movies, and its occult practices. In one hour it will all be over (Ezekiel 33:2-7).
>
> I believe modern Babylon is present-day America, including its corrupt society and its whorish church system. No other nation on earth fits the description in Revelation 18 but America, the world's biggest fornicator with the merchants of all nations. Ancient Babylon was long destroyed when John received this vision. John saw fiery destruction coming in one hour. (See Revelation 18:8-10.)
>
> Just as Israel was called the city of God, America is referred to as Babylon, that mighty city. It is a people, a land. In one hour it is going to be wiped out and consumed by fire. Judgment will fall upon the major cities, the towns, with fire consuming what was once a prosperous, thriving, safe, tranquil land. "And the merchants of the earth shall weep and mourn over her, for no man buyeth their merchandise any more.... And the good things thy soul lusted after are departed from thee... and thou shalt find them no more at all.... For in one hour so great riches is come to nothing" (Revelation 18:11,14,17).[6]

Commenting on the book of Revelation, former Bible teacher and Christian Education Director of the First Presbyterian Church of Hollywood, California, states:

Revelation is the greatest drama of all time. The plot is tense throughout; the final scene is glorious, for Christ comes unto His own. The Hero is our Lord Himself; the villain is the devil. The actors are the seven churches. The characters unloosed by the seals of chapters 6 and 7 are introduced by the "four horsemen." Then those summoned by the trumpets in turn leave the center of the scene of action, and we see the Antichrist, the world ruler, stalking across the stage (chapter 13). This incarnation of the devil himself is determined to set up his own kingdom and be worshiped by men. But Christ brings all to naught. This majestic Actor, bringing His hosts with Him, comes forth— the long-looked-for King of kings and Lord of lords. He drives His enemies from the stage in utter defeat (chapter 19).[7]

Dr. Franklin Logsden reveals Scripture's intention by the mark of the Beast.

The word "mark" occurs eight times in the Bible. All are found in the Revelation and all pertain to the Beast, the Antichrist, and the world power of which he will be the acknowledged head. The word comes from the Greek *charagma*, and means an etching or stamp.... It probably will be pictorial, containing a word slogan. In any event, it most surely will set forth the idea of great prosperity and equal opportunity for all. This is what the world desires, and political leaders are past masters in promising the people what they want. While this prominent person in prophecy is termed a "beast," when he is manifested and is operating, he will have a name. However, the Bible refers not only to the "mark of his name" (Revelation 14:11), but also to the "number of his name" (Revelation 13:17; 15:2). The number is said to be 666, but since it has to be counted (Revelation 13:18) in order to arrive at this figure, the number is apparently arranged in the design of the insignia.[8]

Renowned Bible teacher W. Graham Scroggie lays out the structure of the Revelation this way:

The symbolism of the Book is neither Greek nor Roman, but Hebrew. The originality of the Writing is, for the most part, not in the presentation of new ideas, but in a new combination of old ideas. Almost all of it is traceable in the Old Testament; every figure in it is drawn from the Old Testament. Of its 404 verses, 265 contain Old Testament language, and there are about 550 references to Old Testament passages. But for the Old Testament this Book would remain an utter enigma.

It is related to the New Testament, structurally, chronologically, and spiritually. The subject matter of each Testament is in three groups of Writings, and in the same order, the Historical, Genesis to Esther, and Matthew to Acts: the Didactical, Job to Canticles, and Romans to Jude: and the Prophetical, Isaiah to Malachi, and the Revelation. Matthew to John treats of the past; Acts to Jude of the present; and the Revelation, of the future. In the first group we have the Christ, in the second, the Church, and in the Revelation, the Consummation.

It is related to the Book of Daniel. Daniel treats of four Empires, the Babylonian, Medo-Persian, Grecian, and Roman. Revelation treats of the last of these only. Daniel presents the whole course of the Roman Empire, but the Revelation tells only of the latter end of it.[9]

Speaking of the image in Daniel 3 and Revelation 13, the late M.R. DeHaan states:

To thoroughly understand the prophetic meaning of the image in Daniel 3 and Revelation 13, we must go even farther back in Biblical history. For Babylon and Babylonianism began in the days immediately after the Flood of Noah. We have the record in Genesis 10 and 11. There you will recall a man by the name of Nimrod (meaning "the rebel"), who, like Nebuchadnezzar, was a type of the Antichrist, built the city of Babylon and a great tower, and on the top of this tower he placed the image of his god "Belus" or Baal. This first Babylon or Babel was a picture of Babylon throughout all the ages to follow. For Babel or Babylon is a system, a political and religious system opposed to the true religion of Jehovah. It is Satan's counterfeit of God's kingdom, and whether we see it in the form of the Egyptian Empire, or the Assyrian, or the Babylonian, or the Persian, or the Greek, or the Roman Empire, it is always the same, for it is engineered by the same author, Satan. Babylonianism is an ideology; it is Satan's attempt to set up a kingdom in opposition to the kingdom of our Lord Jesus Christ. It began in ancient Babylon under Nimrod. This man built a great city, one of the wonders of the world, and this city represented a political system. But he also built a tower, which was the seat of Babel's worship of the Babylonian god, and this tower represented a religious system. There was only one language and one government.

Nimrod, the founder of Babel, sought to establish a world empire, a world federation, politically and religiously. To keep men from being divided he devised Babel, by which he attempted to achieve one government, one religion, one language, one United Nations of the World. And so he called it Babel, which means, from the two fragments "Bab" and "El," the "gate to God." It was a false religion, a spurious plan of redemption by man's efforts and man's works.... Nimrod's ancient Babylon was destroyed, though its ruins remain to this day to indicate that the spirit of Babylon still lives on to be revived again and again but always to perish and arise again in another form, but always the same program, a world political federation, a world religious federation and a world language and government.[10]

Dr. Emery Bancroft was noted for his intimate knowledge of the Bible. His *Elemental Theology* was one of my textbooks in Bible school. Regarding the prominence of the second coming of Christ he writes:

This subject, which was so dear to the heart of the early Church and which was so prominent in Apostolic teaching and preaching, has in these days of modern thought and theology been relegated very much to the background. The teaching regarding the Second Coming of Christ has been in the history of the Church very much like the pendulum of a clock, swinging from one extreme to another. In the days when the Apostle Paul wrote his first and second epistles to the church at Thessalonica, the pendulum of this teaching was at one of these extremes, or tending that way. Some seemed to have decided that Christ's coming was so near that the only proper thing for them to do was to give up all work for their subsistence and wait for the sounding of the trumpet announcing the Lord's return; but Paul wrote the second epistle to regulate this pendulum of thought and direct their religious fervor into the proper channels.

After the first few centuries the pendulum began to swing back to the other extreme, and it seems that the religious world almost lost sight of this blessed hope of the Church. This was true during that period which is remembered as the dark ages when popery and priestcraft reigned and even for some time after the Reformation. Then the teaching of the Second Coming began to be revived, the midnight cry was made amid the darkness of superstition and false teaching and the Church began to examine and trim her lamps, and prepare to meet the Bridegroom. . . . In the Old Testament there are by far a greater number of predictions concerning the Second Coming than the first.[11]

Commenting on the Laodicean church (Revelation 3:15, 16), which is the last church of Revelation chapter 3, prior to the Lord's coming, and typical of the church today, Bible background expert William Barclay makes two excellent points.

Verses 15 and 16 go on to say that, because Laodicea is neither cold nor hot but lukewarm, it will be absolutely and totally rejected; and this is said with such crude violence that the intensity of the feeling behind it cannot be mistaken. The word which is used for hot is *zestos*, and *zestos* means more than hot; it means at boiling-point. Here is the great fact that there can be no real religion without enthusiasm. We have seen that Laodicea was a great commercial and trading center; we have seen that it was a very prosperous city. It is very likely that the people of Laodicea drew the line when religion began interfering with their business.

The word for lukewarm is *chliaros*, which means tepid. In the district around Laodicea there were hot mineral springs. A medicinal spring can have a most nauseating taste. It may well be that the picture is taken from these mineral springs, and that the Risen Christ is saying: "Sometimes when a man goes to drink of the medicinal springs, the tepid and the ill-tasting water makes his gorge rise and makes him want to vomit; that is the way in which I feel about a Church that is neither hot or cold." The plain fact is that in Christianity there is no room for neutrality. The person who has not declared for Christ has declared against Christ.[12]

R.C.H. Lenski, a native of Germany, was honored with the D.D. degree in 1915. His commentary on the New Testament is a classic. Because of his proficiency with *koine* Greek he makes every Bible text come alive. In John 14:3 Christ says, "If I go and prepare a place for you, I will come again and receive you to Myself, that where I am, there you may be also." Dr. Lenski writes:

> With this great promise Jesus plants the comfort of hope in his disciples. The translation indicates the assured reading of the text. The [Greek grammer] presents expectancy, but one coupled with certainty: "If I shall go," etc., as indeed I shall. The aorists "shall go and prepare" denote actuality as well as single acts. "Shall go" refers to the ascension of Jesus. "Shall prepare" or "make ready" is a heavenly act.[13]

One of my favorite Bible teachers is Dr. John C. Whitcomb. Dr. Whitcomb tackles the tough issue of Daniel's seventieth week this way:

> The first question that confronts us is the relative chronology. What are the seventy "weeks"? When do they begin and end? This is an example of chronology's providing a key for identity. Space does not allow here the detailed discussion these questions deserve, but all lines of evidence seem to point to the following conclusions: 1) The term "week"

[Heb. *sabua*] refers to a unit of seven, in this context seven years. Therefore the prophecy deals with a time span covering 490 years. 2) The seventy years began to count at the year 445 B.C., when King Artaxerxes gave official permission for Nehemiah to rebuild and fortify Jerusalem. 3) When Messiah is cut off, the seventieth week is postponed (from man's perspective) to the end time, still future to our day, and will be concluded with the second coming of Christ and the destruction of the Antichrist.

It should be noted carefully that the prophecy does not focus on the church but rather on "your people" (Israel) and "your holy city" (Jerusalem). This hermeneutical key unlocks the meaning of large numbers of prophetic Scriptures that have remained obscure during the centuries when Israel and the church have been considered to be essentially the same entity.[14]

For years the voice of J. Vernon McGee filled the religious airways. After a 21-year pastorate at the historic Church of the Open Door in Los Angeles, Dr. McGee preached and taught the Bible around the world. Focusing on Revelation chapter 20 and the teaching of the millennium, he says:

In the twentieth chapter we are dealing with the Millennium in relationship to Christ, Satan, man, the tribulation saints, the resurrections, the earth, and the Great White Throne. Unfortunately, a great many men in the past have thought that chapter 20 is not very important because the Millennium, the thousand-year period, is mentioned only here in Scripture, and therefore, they have practically dismissed this chapter altogether. It is true that the Millennium is mentioned only in this chapter, and it is mentioned as "a thousand years." Let's not argue about semantics. Millennium comes from the Latin word that means "one thousand." Millennium means a thousand years any way you slice it. You can call a person who believes in the Millennium a chiliast, and chiliasm is the way the early church spoke of it, because in the Greek chiliasm means "a thousand" also. I hope we understand that millennialism, chiliasm, and the thousand-year reign of Christ all refer to the same thing.

In the first nine verses of this chapter, we have the word for a thousand years repeated six times. It must be pretty important to put that kind of emphasis on it. The early church believed in what was known as chiliasm, the belief in the literal thousand-year reign of Christ.[15]

The cleanest model of an evangelist in our times, Dr. Billy Graham has pointed the masses to the return of Christ globally.

The promised coming of the Lord has been the great hope of true believers down through the centuries. Emil Brunner once said, "What oxygen is to the lungs, such is hope to the meaning of life." Some years ago in a Telstar discussion, Lord Montgomery asked General Eisenhower, "Can you give any hope?" Mr. Eisenhower prescribed a way out, "which if man misses," he said, "would lead to Armageddon." Winston Churchill's favorite American song was "The Battle Hymn of the Republic," which begins with the stirring phrase, "Mine eyes have see the glory of the coming of the Lord."

The great creeds of the church teach that Christ is coming back. The Nicene Creed states that "He shall come again with glory to judge both the living and the dead." Charles Wesley wrote 7000 hymns, and in 5000 he mentioned the coming of Christ.[16]

Notes

$\blacklozenge$ ══════ $\blacklozenge$

Foreword
1. *The New Jersey Ledger*, Sept. 4, 1991.
2. *Time* magazine, Sept. 9, 1991.

Chapter 2—A Futurist Prophesies What's Ahead
1. Sigurd O. Nielson, "Fan of the Futures," in *The Futurist*, Jan.-Feb. 1991, p. 49.
2. Macvey in *The Futurist*, Nov.-Dec. 1990, p. 39.
3. Veatch in *The Futurist*, Nov.-Dec. 1990, p. 37.
4. Morf in *The Futurist*, Nov.-Dec. 1990, p. 52.
5. Jennifer Jarratt and John B. Mahaffie reporting on Joseph Coates, *Future Work*, in *The Futurist*, May-June 1991, pp. 10-11.
6. *The Futurist*, Nov.-Dec. 1990, p. 56.

Chapter 3—Irrefutable Proofs
1. Josh McDowell, *Evidence That Demands A Verdict* (San Bernardino, CA: Here's Life, 1979), p. 175.
2. Henry M. Morris, *Many Infallible Proofs* (San Diego: Christian Life Publishers, 1979), pp. 14,15,157.
3. Ibid., pp. 22-23.
4. "Personalities," in *The Washington Post*, C3, Jan. 7, 1988.

Chapter 4—Characteristic Days of His Return
1. James Patterson and Peter Kim, *The Day America Told the Truth* (New York: Prentice Hall, 1991), passim.
2. Joe Urschel, "Madonna," in *USA Today*, Friday, May 13, 1991, p. 13-A.
3. Don Shewey, "The Saint, The Slut, The Sensation," in *The Advocate*, May 7, 1991, pp. 48,50; May 21, 1991, pp. 42,44.
4. Anastasia Toufexis, "Struggling for Sanity," in *Time*, Oct. 8, 1990, pp. 47-48.

Chapter 5—Apocalyptic Apostasy
1. Leonard Ravenhill, *Why Revival Tarries* (Minneapolis: Bethany House, 1959), pp. 99-100.

221

2. Jeffery L. Shaler, "Revisiting the Abyss," in *U.S. News & World Report*, March 25, 1991, p. 64.
3. Kenneth L. Woodward, "Heaven," in *Newsweek*, March 27, 1989, page 54.
4. Gustav Niebuhr, "Megachurches Strive to Be All Things to All Parishioners," in *The Wall Street Journal*, May 13, 1991, p. A-1.
5. Kenneth L. Woodward, "A Time to Seek," in *Newsweek*, Dec. 17, 1990, pp. 50-52, 55.
6. Home Mission Board, Evangelism Church Growth Department, 1350 Spring Street, NW, Atlanta, GA 30367-5601.
7. Colin Whittaker, "Britain Believing for a Decade of Harvest," in *Pentecostal Evangel*, April 1991, p. 8.
8. Paul Y. Cho, *Prayer: Key to Revival* (Waco: Word Books, 1984), pp. 14-15, 17.

Chapter 8—Unlocking Daniel's Precise Predictions
1. Charle H. Dyer, *Rise of Babylon* (Wheaton, IL: Tyndale House, 1991), pp. 26-27.
2. Joyce C. Baldwin, *Daniel*, in *Tyndale Old Testament Commentaries* (InterVarsity Press, 1978), p. 80.
3. *Wycliffe Bible Commentary* (New York: The Iversen-Norman Associates, 1975), p. 53.
4. John F. Walvoord, *Daniel: A Commentary* (Chicago: Moody Press, 1971), p. 161.

Chapter 9—Satan's Superman
1. *Miami Review*, Thursday, July 2, 1981, p. 7.
2. Michael Rogers, "Smart Cards: Pocket Power," in *Newsweek*, July 31, 1989, p. 54.

Chapter 11—The Occultic Bonanza
1. George Gallup, Jr. and Jim Castelli, "For Many the Devil Is Reality," in *The Kansas City Star*, Aug. 25, 1990, p. E-1.
2. "Our Violent Kids," in *Time*, June 12, 1989.
3. Miro Cernetig, "Something evil lurks in the heart of Alberta Bible Belt," in *The Globe and Mail*, Mar. 23, 1990, p. A9.
4. Peter Howell, "In Twin Peaks, Satan is a hometown boy," in *The Toronto Star*, Oct. 13, 1990, p. F3.

Chapter 12—Deceptive Preconditioning
1. "Child-Rearing in a New Age," in *St. Paul Pioneer Press Dispatch*, May 27, 1989.

Chapter 15—The Awaiting Glory
1. *Ebony*, Oct. 1990, p. 54.

Chapter 16—The Greats Sound Off!
1. John F. Walvoord, *The Church in Prophecy* (Grand Rapids: Zondervan, 1964).
2. Charles Hodge, *Systematic Theology* (Wm. B. Eerdmans, reprinted 1977), pp. 803-04.
3. J. Oliver Buswell, *A Systematic Theology of the Christian Religion*, Vol. One (Grand Rapids: Zondervan, 1962).
4. William Evans, *The Great Doctrines of the Bible* (Chicago: Moody Press, 1912), pp. 303-04.
5. W.A. Criswell, *Welcome Back, Jesus!* (Broadman Press, 1976), pp. 86,87.
6. David Wilkerson, *Set the Trumpet to Thy Mouth* (Lindale, TX: World Challenge, Inc.), pp. 1-4.
7. Henrietta C. Mears, *What the Bible Is All About* (Glendale, CA: Gospel Light Publications, 1953), p. 651.
8. S. Franklin Logsden, *Profiles in Prophecy* (Bowdon Publications, 1964), pp. 75-76.
9. W. Graham Scroggie, *Know Your Bible* (Fleming H. Revell, 1940), pp. 372-73.
10. M.R. DeHaan, *Daniel the Prophet* (Grand Rapids: Zondervan, 1947), pp. 74-76.
11. Emery H. Bancroft, *Elemental Theology* (Grand Rapids: Zondervan, 1960), pp. 275-76.
12. William Barclay, *Letters to Seven Churches* (London: SCM Press, 1957), pp. 116-17.
13. R.C.H. Lenski, *The Interpretation of St. John's Gospel* (Augsburg Publishing House, 1943), p. 973.
14. John C. Whitcomb, *Daniel* (Chicago: Moody Press, 1985), p. 129.
15. J. Vernon McGee, *Thru the Bible, 1 Corinthians—Revelation* (Thomas Nelson, 1983), pp. 1052-53).
16. Billy Graham, *Approaching Hoofbeats: The Four Horsemen of the Apocalypse* (Waco, TX: Word, 1983), p. 210.

Glossary of Terms

✦ ══════════════ ✦

This is not an exhaustive treatment of eschatological terms, but the understanding of certain key terms is very important for everyone seeking to comprehend end-times prophecy.

Advent—coming, referring to Christ. His first coming was as a suffering Savior (Isaiah 53). His second coming will be as the victorious, all-conquering Son of God (Matthew 24:30).

Angel—messenger of God (see Daniel) and aiding spirit to those who are redeemed (Hebrews 1:14).

Antichrist—the infamous evil opponent of Jesus Christ (Revelation 13; 2 Thessalonians 2:3-9).

Apocalyptic—Jewish and Christian inspired writings which through their employment of signs, symbols, visions, and dreams have specific future predictions. (Main examples are the books of Daniel and Revelation).

Day of the Lord—the decisive moment in future history when Christ will return to this planet with sin judged and righteousness established eternally.

Demons—evil spirits, subjected to Satan, originally angels of God who fell due to disobedience (Isaiah 14:11-15; Ezekiel 28:12-19).

Devil—leader of wicked spirits in constant rebellion against God. He will energize the Antichrist for the ultimate reign of terror (Revelation 13; 1 Peter 5:8).

Eschatology—study of the last things or end times when Christ returns.

Evangelism—principal mission of the church to proclaim God's love and forgiveness to lost people of all nations before the end of the world (Matthew 28:19,20).

Exile—life in a foreign nation away from one's homeland, generally the result of military defeat.

Glorification—a future reality for every Christian, when our bodies will be transformed at the coming of Jesus Christ to become sinless, perfect, and incapable of sickness or trauma (Philippians 3:20,21).

Heaven—the future, literal, perfect, eternal home prepared for those who have been born again by faith in Christ (John 14:1-3).

Hell—the literal place of punishment of those who reject Jesus Christ as Lord and Savior (John 3:36).

Heresy—any teaching which denies, distorts, or attempts to undermine the literal application of God's Word.

Judgment—God's work at the end of the age, including punishment for the lost and rewards for the redeemed (Matthew 24,25).

Martyr—one who because of his faith in and allegiance to Christ is killed (see Revelation 7:9,10).

Millennium—glorious period after Christ's second coming to the earth when He will reign on this planet for 1000 years (Revelation 20:1-6).

Parable—a short story from everyday life used to illustrate an eternal truth.

Paraclete—Greek word for Helper or Comforter, referring to the Holy Spirit, indwelt in every believer at the moment of conversion (Romans 8:9).

Parousia—Greek word meaning "coming" or "presence," used to refer to Christ's coming, particularly His second coming (1 Corinthians 1:8; 2 Thessalonians 2:8).

Pentecost—the actual beginning of the church (Acts 2) on the fiftieth day after Passover.

Rapture—the coming of Christ for His saints, when they will be snatched away to meet Him in the air (1 Thessalonians 4:13-18).

Saints—any person who has accepted Jesus Christ as personal Lord and Savior.

Scripture—the Bible, God's holy, infallible, inerrant Word, comprised of 66 books divided into the Old and New Testaments.

Other Good Harvest House Reading

GLOBAL PEACE AND THE RISE OF ANTICHRIST
by *Dave Hunt*

Noted author and researcher Dave Hunt pieces together world affairs and offers a biblical analysis of how global events could be setting the stage for history's final conflict. Hunt powerfully emphasizes that the study of prophecy is meant to stir our love for Jesus into active passion and to enrich our lives as we await His return.

HOW TO STUDY THE BIBLE FOR YOURSELF
by *Tim LaHaye*

This excellent book provides fascinating study helps and charts that will make personal Bible study more interesting and exciting. A three-year program is outlined for a good working knowledge of the Bible.

PEACE, PROSPERITY AND THE COMING HOLOCAUST
by *Dave Hunt*

With fresh insight and vision, Dave Hunt dissects the influences that are at work to lull us into a state of euphoria and numb us to the reality of coming destruction. A startling account of the rapidly growing New Age Movement and the part it plays in the imminent return of Jesus Christ.

ONE WORLD UNDER ANTICHRIST
by *Peter Lalonde*

Author Peter Lalonde takes you into the stories behind the news, and examines how these events are connected to each other and to the much-talked-about New World Order. Highly readable and well-documented, *One World Under Antichrist* cuts through the confusion while offering hope and challenge for the Christian who wants a deeper understanding of last days' events.